ENNEAGRAM

*A Practical Guide to Understanding Yourself
and Others Based on the
9 Primary and
27 Associated Personality Types
(2022 Guide for Beginners)*

Kyla Wilkinson

ENNEAGRAM

Contents

Introduction 1

Chapter 1: The Enneagram Theory 3

Chapter 2: The Overachiever 15

Chapter 3: The Assistant 25

Chapter 4: The Winner 34

Chapter 5: The Independentist 44

Chapter 6: The Detective 56

Chapter 7: The Loyalist Party 64

Chapter 8: The Passionate 72

Chapter 9: The Defender 79

Chapter 10: The Arbiter 88

Chapter 11: Testing 97

Conclusion 102

INTRODUCTION

This book contains detailed descriptions of nine different types of personalities. The Enneagram theory is made up of these personalities. You will gain a better understanding of not only yourself, but also of your friends, partners, family, and coworkers as a result of these personalities.

This book can help you get started on your path to self-discovery. You will learn your strengths and weaknesses, as well as how to turn your weaknesses into strengths. You will discover your personality's highs and lows. All of this information will assist you in becoming the best person you can be.

This book begins by explaining the Enneagram theory.

You'll see a few of its diagrams, including the Enneagram and its center points. You will be given a brief overview of the nine personality types and the 27 subtypes, as each personality type has three subtypes. You will also discover the advantages of the Enneagram theory.

Beginning in chapter 2, you will learn about the various types of individual personalities. We'll start with the first personality type, the perfectionist. The helper will be discussed in Chapter 3. In Chapter 4, we will investigate the achiever. The individualist, the fourth personality type, will be discussed in Chapter 5. The fifth personality type, the investigator, will be discussed in Chapter 6. In Chapter 7, I will discuss the loyalist or the sixth personality type. The enthusiast, the seventh personality type, will be discussed in Chapter 8. The protector will be discussed in Chapter 9. Finally, in Chapter 10, we'll look at the ninth personality type, the mediator or peacemaker.

Chapter 11 is a special chapter because it focuses on the Enneagram test, which is available online for free. However, you can always take the time and spend the money to take the test somewhere else. This chapter will describe the test, provide a summary of the types and subtypes, and explain the distinction between the Enneagram and the Myer-Briggs test.

By the end of this book, you should have a basic understanding of the Enneagram theory. You should be able to identify not only your personality type but also your strengths, weaknesses, and how you interact with other personalities. This book will also help you determine whether you have a healthy, average, or unhealthy level of integration. You will be able to find ways to help you reach the healthiest level once you have identified your level, allowing you to become the best person you can be.

The Enneagram is more than just a personality test that tells you what number you are. It is a test that can provide you with the information you require to ensure that you are living your life to the fullest. At this point, I believe it is critical that you understand that everyone makes mistakes and that no one is perfect.

There are a couple of Enneagram personalities who struggle with flaws. If you identify with one of these personalities, the first step is to accept that it is okay to be wrong, to struggle, and to not always be happy. However, it is also critical to keep your mindset in mind. Whatever personality you have, you must maintain a positive frame of mind if you want to maintain a healthy level of personality.

CHAPTER 1

The Enneagram Theory

Nobody knows for certain where the Enneagram theory originated. Some believe it can be traced back mathematically, while others believe it began with spirituality and Christianity. Plotinus, a 200 A.D. Greek philosopher, spoke of nine principles of human personality. Ramon Llull, a 13th-century mathematician, also discussed nine personality types (Cloete, n.d.).

However, no matter how far back you go in time, you will find an evolution devoted to the Enneagram theory. The Enneagram theory is now a diagram used to determine a person's personality. Many psychologists, however, have used this theory to identify people in large groups (Cloete, n.d.).

How Does It Work?

One of the unique aspects of the Enneagram theory is that it does not categorize people. There are 27 subtypes of personalities within the nine major types. In addition, each personality has wings, lines, and other characteristics that contribute to your distinct personality (Cloete, n.d.). While the theory and diagram may appear complicated at first, as they are, it becomes easier to understand as you learn more about the types, subtypes, and how the theory works in general.

The Enneagram
The Three Centers of Intelligence

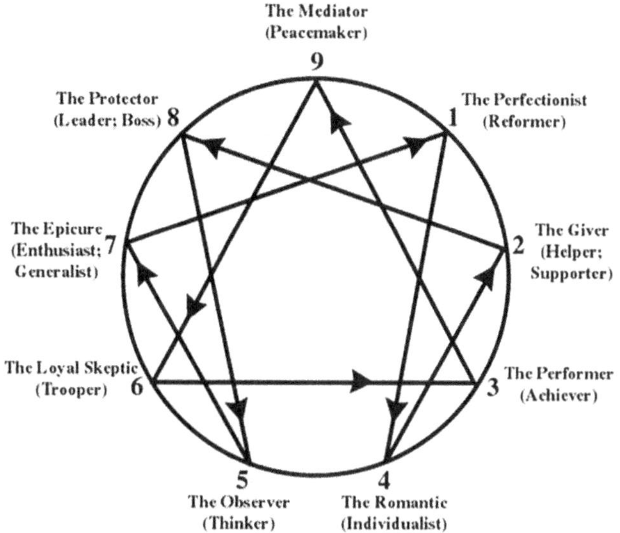

You will want to look at the Enneagram diagram step by step to help you understand it. This will help you better understand and follow the Enneagram's basic structure. For example, you could begin by viewing the diagram as a circle. The numbers nine through one can be found around this circle. While the numbers are numerical, they are also placed in a systematic order if you go counter-clockwise, which is why nine is at the top. Each of these nine numbers represents a different personality type, as shown in the diagram above.

People frequently become perplexed by the lines within the circle. As you can see, several lines connect one number to the next. These are the lines that will lead you to your personality and its wings. Again, reading the lines one by one will help you better understand the Enneagram.

First, consider the numbers nine, six, and three. When you connect them, you will notice that they form an equilateral triangle. From there, examine the connections of numbers through six points that form an irregular hexagram. You must follow the order listed below because the points must be completed in this order.

1. The number 1 is linked to the number 4.
2. The number 4 is linked to the number 2.
3. The number 2 is linked to the number 8.
4. The number 8 is linked to the number 5.
5. The number 5 is linked to the number 7.
6. The number 7 is related to the number 1.

When you look at the lines in the Enneagram, you will notice arrows that lead to the following number.

There are 9 types and 27 subtypes.

You should never believe that your personality will fit into a single category. You will find elements of your personality in every other personality. You should, however, look for the primary number associated with your personality. This number will represent the most important aspect of your personality. Remember that the Enneagram is designed to take you out of a box, not put you in one.

As a result, your personality will be dispersed throughout the diagram, but you will only have one primary number.

In this section, I'll go over the nine personality types and 27 subtypes that can make up your personality. This section will not go into detail about these types and subtypes. Instead, the following chapters will be dedicated to each of the nine types, where I will go into greater detail about the types, subtypes, and other factors.

The Enneagram's nine personality types are as follows (Berkers, n.d.):

1. The Overachiever
2. The Assistant
3. The Winner
4. The Independentist
5. The Detective
The Loyalists
7. The Passionate
8. The Defender
The Mediator (9)

Within these nine personality types, there are a total of 27 subtypes.

These subtypes are organized into three major categories. These are social, self-preservation, and one-on-one interactions (Cloete, n.d.).

The social category is concerned with how we interact with others and our social instincts. It describes how we maintain relationships and collaborate with others. The social category is also concerned with how we strive to do our best for others (Cloete, n.d.).

The self-preservation category is concerned with how well we protect our bodies and minds. It has to do with how we deal with stress and other life events. It is the category that is concerned with our emotions. This category examines how we can do our best to protect ourselves mentally, physically, and emotionally (Cloete, n.d.).

The one-on-one category is concerned with the legacies we wish to leave for future generations. Everyone wants to be remembered when they die, whether they are in your family or around the world. This category focuses on how we deal with these kinds of situations.

It delves deeper into our more personal one-on-one interactions with people as well as environmental factors. This category allows us to decide what we want to leave behind and how we want to live our lives while still on this planet (Cloete, n.d.).

Within the social, self-preservation, and one-on-one categories, each personality type has one subtype. Because this is a complex subject, I will list each personality type, along with its category and subtype, below. I'll go over each subtype in more detail later.

1. The Perfectionist Social: Inflexible
Worrying about one's survival: Zeal

2. The Aspirational Helper Social
Privilege of self-preservation
Seduction one-on-one

3. The Achiever Social: Prestige
Self-preservation: Security Charisma One-on-one:

4. Shame in the Individualist Social
Tenacity in self-preservation
Competition in one-on-one situations

5. The Investigator Social:
Totem Self-preservation: Castle Confident one-on-one

6. Duty at the Loyalist Social
Warmth Self-preservation: Intimidation One-on-one

7. The Enthusiast Social: Making a Sacrifice
Networking for self-preservation
One-on-one: Interest

8. The Social Protector: Solidarity
Self-preservation: Contentment

9. Possession one-on-one
Participation in the Mediator Social
Appetite for self-preservation
Fusion, one-on-one

Points of Interest

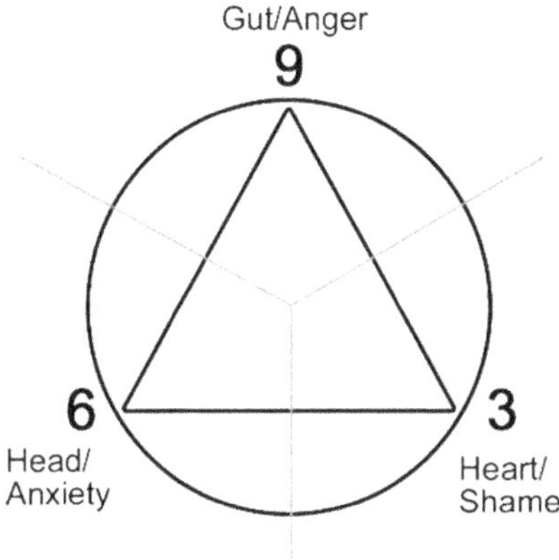

Aside from the numbers and lines, the diagram is divided into three triads or centers: heart, head, and body. These centers will help you develop your personality further by explaining your primary emotions.

The heart center is concerned with the numbers four, three, and two. Because the heart is often thought to be the leader of truth and emotions, these numbers usually represent someone who is more sensitive and believes that we must be honest about who we are.

Individuals who fall into the heart center have a strong connection to the truth.

Shame is the default emotion for the heart center. They are preoccupied with their image and how others perceive them. They are never truly satisfied with themselves unless they can see themselves through the eyes of another person.

The heart center, like the other two centers, has strengths and weaknesses; however, these strengths and weaknesses are determined by your personality type. Type four's strengths, for example, will differ from type two's ("Heart Triad," n.d.).

Points for wings

The wing points are the aspects of your personality that spread to your two neighboring personality types (Cloete, n.d.). While these two personality types are not as significant as your primary personality type, they are significant because they will balance out your personality. If you have a point four personality type, your adjacent type could be a point three. These other types are sometimes known to contradict a person's personality, but they are necessary so that we can fully understand someone's personality. This is why tests and theories like the Enneagram exist. It not only helps us get to know ourselves better, but it can also help people like psychologists who are trying to get to know us so they can help us.

Many people are curious as to whether we all have one or two wings. While this has caused some debate, many people believe that we do have two wings. One of our wings is each point adjacent to our primary personality type. As a result, if you are a type nine, your wings will be type one and type eight.

Others, however, claim that this is not true and that everyone has only one wing. Others argue that your wings are not limited to a particular personality type. They believe that because our personalities contain elements from each number, we have the main type and each other type is a wing to our personality, giving us eight wings.

One thing to keep in mind about having different wings is that some are more dominant than others. If you haven't taken the Enneagram test yet, you'll notice that your results are presented in a graph. This graph begins with your strongest personality and then lists the other types of personalities in order of strength. The majority of the results will include all nine personality types.

Lines

The lines within the theory are one of the most difficult aspects of the Enneagram theory for people to grasp. While I have previously discussed the lines, such as how they connect to the point, I will take this opportunity to provide you with additional information about what the lines mean.

These are known as lines of influence or lines of movement (Cloete, n.d.). They will guide you through the Enneagram to determine your personality type. Even though we have a dominant personality type, we can shift between them. Our main type will remain the same; however, the situations we face in life and other factors will influence our journey along the Enneagram lines.

Lines are classified into two types. There is a stress line and a growth line. When you look at your Enneagram main personality type, you will notice two lines with arrows. The line of growth is represented by one arrow pointing away from your number type. The other arrow will point to your number type, and this is known as the line of stress.

When you consider the path of development, you may consider releasing yourself from your unhealthy personality types. This is the line that leads us to the more positive aspects of our personalities. As we progress along this path, we will be able to release our life stresses and move closer to self-actualization (Cloete, n.d.).

The stress line is the inverse of the growth line. This line is about how we feel when we are under stress or pressure.

These situations frequently lead to the development of unhealthy lifestyle habits. Simultaneously, we can work to turn negatives into positives, which will often help us balance out as individuals (Cloete, n.d.).

Integration Levels

Levels of integration are also known as integration levels. Other components make up the personality within each personality type. These are comparable to your actions, motivations, and attitude. Essentially, these are the pieces that contribute to your overall personality, much like how puzzle pieces come together to form the whole puzzle.

When you begin to understand these levels, you will notice that when people change, such as feeling more relaxed one moment and anxious the next, they are transitioning through different levels of their personality.

There are three integration levels: healthy, average, and unhealthy (Cloete, n.d.). People who have an unhealthy level of integration allow their fears or other emotions to control them. When people reach an average level of integration, the core problem continues to drive their behavior, but they can let go of some core issues. People who have reached a healthy level of integration can let go of their core emotions because they understand why they are happening. This allows them to move on and find a healthier way to deal with life's stresses and situations. In a sense, they transcend the boundaries they thought they had.

Other levels and numbers are associated with each of these levels of integration. Each level is assigned three numbers that represent how well the personality performs within its level of integration. These are the smaller levels:

You can be a level one, two, or three in the healthy level. Level one is that of a libertarian. Level two is about psychological capacity, and level three is about social value ("How the System Works," n.d.).

You can be a level four, five, or six on average. Level four represents the social role or imbalance. Level five is about interpersonal control. Level six is the overcompensation level ("How the System Works," n.d.).

You can be a level seven, eight, or nine in the unhealthy level. Level seven is a violation level. Level eight is characterized by compulsion and obsession. Level nine represents pathological destructiveness ("How the System Works," n.d.).

The Enneagram's Advantages

People frequently use the Enneagram to learn more about their personality for a variety of reasons. While some people are interested in their personality type, others want to know to better understand themselves or another person. The Enneagram is frequently used by psychologists and other professionals to help them better understand their patients.

The Enneagram can provide several advantages.

This theory and test can benefit people not only individually, but also as a group. Furthermore, the Enneagram can help people on a professional level.

Individual Advantages

Assist people in understanding why they are experiencing certain behavioral or emotional issues.

Assist people in gaining insight into their personalities so that they can better understand themselves.

The Enneagram can help people gain confidence and motivation.

The Enneagram can help people develop more compassion for others.

People can begin to comprehend their prior behavioral patterns.

The Enneagram can help people grow in general by helping them better understand their personalities.

Benefits at the Group Level

The Enneagram can help reduce group conflict.

It can also assist each group member in understanding where another group member stands, why people act the way they do, and where each member's strengths and weaknesses are.

The Enneagram can aid in the improvement of business processes.

It can improve communication among team members, which will benefit other areas of the group.

Benefits at the Organizational Level

The Enneagram can help limit an organization's political atmosphere.

It has the potential to improve the overall leadership of the organization.

The Enneagram can assist the organization in better managing the emotions and fears associated with change.

The Enneagram is much more than a line, number, and arrow diagram. It can also do more than just describe someone's personality. As evidenced by the benefits listed above, the Enneagram can help people advance in a variety of areas of their personal and professional lives. Furthermore, the Enneagram can continue to assist you as you progress through the stages of life.

CHAPTER 2

The Overachiever

The perfectionist, also known as the reformer, is the first personality type. Every personality type has a set of words that accurately describe it. While you should always read through your personality type description, these few words can also give you an idea of your personality. Perfectionists are described as perfectionistic, self-controlled, purposeful, and principled.

What exactly is the Perfectionist?

People associate the term perfectionist with someone who is driven, and controlling, and needs to ensure that everything is always perfect. While all of this is true for this personality type, as with all others, there are different levels of integration. These levels indicate the degree to which a person's personality is healthy or unhealthy. For example, someone with an unhealthy level of perfectionist personality will not listen to someone who contradicts what he or she believes. However, if the type two personality is functioning normally, the perfectionist personality is tolerant, accepting, and understands that while he or she wishes to be as perfect as possible, perfection is unattainable ("Type One," n.d.).

The true meaning of a type one personality is that they have a strong sense of what is right and wrong. They understand rules and ethics and believe they should be strictly adhered to. At the same time, they want to see positive change and will do whatever they believe is necessary to bring about that change ("Type One," n.d.).

People with type one personalities are terrified of making mistakes. This is why they frequently take longer to complete a task.

They must ensure that everything is done as perfectly as possible to limit mistakes. They frequently believe that everything must be done in a specific order and can maintain high standards.

Their flaws include a lack of patience, becoming overly controlling, and being resentful ("Type One," n.d.).

Corruption is the perfectionist's worst nightmare. While there are numerous reasons for this, one of the most important is that they perceive corruption to be disorderly and uncontrollable. When corruption exists, ethical standards are not followed, and conditions do not improve ("Type One," n.d.).

A perfectionist's greatest desire is to be the best person possible. The perfectionist aspires to be a good person in general, even if he or she has impatient personality traits and withdraws from others. These characteristics are frequently used as a defense mechanism to assist the type one in managing their perfectionist traits.

Type one desires to live in a well-balanced world.

Katherine Hepburn, Maggie Smith, Tina Fey, Hilary Clinton, Michelle Obama, Joan of Arc, Nelson Mandela, Jerry Seinfeld, Prince

Charles, Jimmy Carter, and Kate Middleton are all known type one personalities ("Type One," n.d.).

People with type one personalities are driven by a sense of purpose. They not only have a mission to focus on, but they will also go to any length to complete it. Simultaneously, they feel compelled to justify their actions to themselves.

They will accomplish this by conducting research and asking themselves why this mission is important. If they decide their actions are justified, they become very passionate about making changes.

The type one personality will rarely deviate from their mission or responsibilities ("Type One," n.d.). As a result, they may become resentful of others or their circumstances. This can make the perfectionist appear controlling and incapable of adapting to his or her surroundings. However, this is not always the case. Because perfectionist is constantly striving to improve their circumstances, they become frustrated and either act aggressively or become resentful. This is how many types one personality deal with difficulties, mistakes, and the realization that the situation is out of their hands.

Integration Level

As previously stated, all personalities have varying degrees of integration. These are divided into three categories: healthy, average, and unhealthy. Within these levels, there are smaller levels ranging from one to nine. Levels one through three constitute the healthy level.

Levels four through six are considered moderate, while levels seven through nine are considered unhealthy. A level one personality is a type one personality at its best. Of course, the level will rise or fall depending on how the type one personality handles his or her environmental situations. This means that when a personality reaches an unhealthy level, such as nine, it is at its worst.

Level of Health

When a type one personality is at level one, they are at their peak performance. They have discovered ways to manage their stress in stressful situations, which prevents them from becoming overly aggressive and controlling. While they do not always manage everything perfectly, they understand that this is fine because perfection does not exist.

This, however, will not deter them from trying again. They also recognize that they have no control over the environment or what other people do. As a result, when things don't go as planned, they feel more at ease. They believe that as long as they give their all, they will be successful. They understand that as long as they remain present, they will be able to see and tell the truth to others (Cloete, n.d.).

Perfectionists at the level two healthy level work hard to improve themselves because they know they can do better. Type one will know what is right and wrong at this level. Furthermore, they will understand ethics in all contexts, from work ethics to religious ethics. They are steadfast in their moral values and strive to become self-disciplined. They are also very responsible, mature, and rational in the face of adversity ("Type One," n.d.).

A level three type one is not as healthy. In most situations, they still maintain a healthy way of controlling their aggression.

They strive to do their best in the future. They are rational and concerned with ethics and ensuring that they are followed. These levels make excellent teachers because they believe they have a higher purpose to ensure that others see the truth. They also believe in justice, even when it comes to state and federal laws ("Type One," n.d.).

Level Average

Level four is the highest level for a type one under the average level. People at this level do not always have complete control over their emotions. They believe that it is their responsibility to improve society's conditions, and they are very passionate about this belief.

Unlike healthy perfectionists, they do not always think rationally about their actions and can become resentful or aggressive at times. This is usually demonstrated by telling people that what they are doing is incorrect and explaining how things should be done instead (Cloete, n.d.).

A perfectionist at level five is commonly referred to as a "workaholic." They work hard to keep everything in order, including their emotions. While they do tend to become overly emotional, especially when they make mistakes, they work hard to keep these emotions hidden from others. They, like most perfectionists, have a strong sense of what is right and wrong, but they can also be impressionable. This can lead them to follow people who will not help them achieve their goals, and as a result, they will make mistakes. When this occurs, the type can become resentful (Cloete, n.d.).

A level six perfectionist has strong opinions and is harsh on both others and themselves. At the lowest average level, type one personalities do not monitor their reactions as closely as other perfectionists do. As a result, they are frequently perceived as angry and impatient. Furthermore, they are known to chastise those they believe are wrongdoing. These perfectionists prefer to have things done their way and do not believe that any other method is acceptable (Cloete, n.d.).

Unhealthy Concentration

Level seven is an unhealthy level for a type one personality. People in this category are frequently referred to as bullies. They are people who believe that no one else is correct except themselves. Perfectionists at this level are sometimes referred to as narcissists. When things aren't going as they should, they can become very angry and impatient ("Type One," n.d.).

A level eight perfectionist is frequently so focused on what other people are doing wrong that they lose sight of what they are doing wrong themselves. When this occurs, they may find themselves doing the opposite of what they believe is correct. They are illogical thinkers who have difficulty problem-solving because they do what they believe is right rather than what is right.

They lack the clarity of morals and values that other type one personalities have ("Type One," n.d.).

A type one at its lowest level of integration is represented by a level nine. They struggle in a variety of areas for a variety of reasons.

At this level, some perfectionists are diagnosed with mental illnesses such as severe depression and obsessive-compulsive disorder. Unfortunately, suicidal ideation and suicide are also prevalent at this level (Cloete, n.d.).

Subtypes of the Perfectionist Social Category are as follows:

Non-Adaptable Perfectionists are immobile because they adhere to the rules and morals of what is right. They also believe it is their responsibility to make things right if they see them as wrong, and they are not usually flexible in this regard. One of their primary motivations for making things right is to ensure fairness (Cloete, n.d.).

Worry is in the Self-Preservation Category.

Perfectionists worry a lot because they want to make sure everything they do and everything around them is correct. As a result, they are concerned not only about their actions, but also about the actions of others. This can make them nervous, especially if they believe things aren't going as planned. Part of this is because they need to ensure that they are well-prepared for their current situations. This includes not only ensuring that everything is in order but also noticing every single detail that other people may overlook (Cloete, n.d.).

The One-on-One Category Zeal

Zeal is referred to as a countertype. How well a type one personality manages personal relationships is determined by their healthy, average, and unhealthy levels. Because many people believe they are correct, they feel empowered to tell others they are incorrect. When it comes to close relationships, this can frequently lead to all kinds of conflict (Cloete, n.d.).

Relationships with People of Other Types

Every other personality type is compatible with type one. They can work with any type of person they come into contact with. Of course, each personality will bring its strengths and weaknesses to the relationship. For example, when a type one works with another type one, they frequently clash because they both strongly believe that only one of them is correct. As a result, if they cannot agree on anything, they will struggle to find a happy medium. Perfectionists get along well with personality types nine, two, five, seven, and eight. They will have more difficulty with types one, three, four, and six. All of this, however, is dependent on the level of integration with which one associate, as well as the level of integration with which the other personality type associates ("Relationships (Type Combinations)," n.d.).

Types of Wings

The perfectionist has two wing personalities: type nine and type two. Both of these wings will provide positives and challenges to the perfectionist. The benefits of type nine are their drive, which assists perfectionists in becoming more relaxed, becoming more considerate of others, and understanding that other people can also be correct.

One of the difficulties that type nine brings to type one is that they may ignore difficult situations and thus self-neglect.

The benefits that type two brings to the perfectionist include self-care, helping others, and compassion for others. The difficulties that type two can bring to type one include a sense of being taken advantage of and becoming overly sensitive to what others think of them (Cloete, n.d.).

The Center of Attention

A type one personality is associated with the body center (Cloete, n.d.). You will internalize your anger if you have a type one personality.

People with type one personalities are extremely self-critical and often overly harsh on themselves. They don't harshly criticize themselves because they lack criticism; they do so because they don't want to show their anger to others. They frequently go out of their way to avoid expressing anger toward others.

Strengths of type one:
Hard-working
Honest \sIndependent
Reliable \sAccountable
Type one's flaws include:
Rigidness
Overly-critical

Judgmental \sResentful
Personal Development

Whether you believe you are at or near the highest level of integration, there is always room for personal growth in your professional and personal life. Listed below are several pieces of advice that can help you grow as a type one personality.

Maintain a Positive Attitude

While this will take time, the amount of time depends on your current level. Naturally, the higher the level, the longer it will take. When I talk about having the right mindset, I mean having patience for others, remaining calm, and keeping your emotions in check. Furthermore, most type one personalities believe they are always correct, which can cause them to become emotional if others do not follow their lead or prove them wrong.

Perfectionists are well-known for being excellent teachers. However, they frequently struggle with teaching because they lack patience and consideration for those who make mistakes. However, if you have the right mindset, you will discover that you can be an exceptional teacher; you will just need to ensure that you have the patience, can deal with people who make mistakes, understand that you are not always correct, and understand that perfectionism is not entirely possible. While achieving all of these factors may appear impossible to you, particularly if you have a lower level of integration, you do have the motivation and drive to succeed if you become passionate about acquiring the right mindset.

You'll want to keep your cool. Perfectionists frequently struggle with controlling their emotions. Many perfectionists struggle with controlling their emotions because they are so rigid about how things should be done. Their primary emotion is anger, so they will express it more than any other emotion. This may exacerbate the problems that have already arisen.

As a result, the calmer you can maintain, the better you will be at controlling your emotions, particularly anger. When you can control your anger, you will find it easier to control other emotions (Cloete, n.d.).

CHAPTER 3

The Assistant

The helper and giver personality type is known as type two. This personality type is concerned with helping others. People-pleaser, demonstrative, possessive, and generous are some of the primary words used to describe the helper. The helper's stress line shifts from type two to type eight, while the growth line shifts from type two to type four.

What exactly is the Helper?

Type two personalities include Stevie Wonder, Danny Glover, Martin Sheen, Elizabeth Taylor, and Richard Thomas (John Boy Walton). Individuals with this personality type are typically warm and caring. They are not only generous but also compassionate and do not pass judgment. They are motivated by a desire to assist others and are frequently found in professions such as non-profits and volunteering at soup kitchens ("Type Two," n.d.).

A type two's greatest desire is to be loved, while their greatest fear is feeling unwanted or unloved. One of the primary reasons they focus on helping others is to satisfy this desire. They believe that the more they assist others, the more people will enjoy and care about them. It is this feeling that drives helpers to devote so much time to ensure they are fulfilling their mission of assisting others.

People notice right away that type two personalities have big hearts.

As a result, they are drawn to those who can assist them. Unfortunately, this can also cause issues because many people are more interested in taking advantage of those who are willing to help. This becomes a problem for many type two personalities because they lack the courage to defend themselves against people who take advantage of them. While some can defend themselves, many others continue to help people because they are afraid that if they do not, people will dislike them.

Individuals with type two personalities are like sponges. They tend to absorb other people's emotions, which can make them feel overwhelmed by all the different emotions. If they don't know how to express their emotions, they may be prone to emotional outbursts as a way to relieve stress. As a result, they must strike a balance between feeling loved by others and loving themselves. No amount of love you receive from someone else can ever replace self-love.

Integration Levels

Healthy Level A level one type two is the highest level you can achieve. These people never believe that they should be compensated for their efforts. People who reach this level are known to be selfless and generous because they have true unconditional love for others, including those who have wronged them or others in the past. They consider it a privilege to be accepted by others and to be a part of their lives (Cloete, n.d.).

Level two type two is similar to level one, but these types believe that they should be able to help others. While they are extremely warm, compassionate, and caring people, they also have a more realistic view of how others can take advantage of them. However, they do not always act when they believe they are being exploited ("Type Two," n.d.).

A level three type two tends to care for themselves as much as they do for others. They prefer to strike a balance, but if it comes down to helping themselves or another person, they will choose the latter. They are nurturing, warm, caring, and generous, just like the higher type two personalities.

They believe that everyone has the best intentions (Cloete, n.d.).

Level Average

A level four type two will have many helpful characteristics and good intentions. They frequently do not believe they are entitled to assistance from others. They do, however, brag about how helpful they are.

They believe that people should recognize and reward their actions. However, they do not frequently seek materialistic rewards; instead, they would prefer to be rewarded through praise (Cloete, n.d.).

A level five type two personality expects a return from those they assist. Level five people are also so eager to help others that they can come across as pushy rather than helpful (Cloete, n.d.). They are unable to distinguish between being helpful and becoming overly helpful.

When assisting others, a level six type two personality can become overbearing (Cloete, n.d.). They believe they are deserving of rewards, but they are not always open about this belief. They have a strong sense of self-importance and believe they are irreplaceable.

Unhealthy Concentration

When a helper reaches level seven, they are frequently manipulative.

While they still enjoy assisting others, they now feel more entitled to do so (Cloete, n.d.). For example, if a type two personality assists you with raking your lawn, he or she will inform you of the amount you owe him or her the next time they require or desire something. Unlike healthy-level type twos, this unhealthy level frequently believes that he or she should not perform any actions for free. In some ways, level seven type twos always want something in return for their helpful behavior.

A level eight type two is similar to a level seven, but they frequently believe they are entitled to any type of favor they desire from others (Cloete, n.d.). These favors can include money, housework, or sexual activities. Someone with a type two personality who ranks at level eight is not afraid to ask for what they want.

Furthermore, when they ask for help, they lack the warm and caring personality that the majority of type two personalities have.

The lowest level that a type two personality can have is level nine. They, like the other unhealthy levels, believe they are entitled to favors and jobs done by others (Cloete, n.d.).

However, because of their helpful personality, they will justify their behavior and the way they treat people. They believe that because they treat people with kindness, they can treat people however they want.

Subtypes of Helpers

Ambition is a social category.

Type two personalities are ambitious and frequently take on leadership roles. They like to feel important and needed, so they will seek out people and organizations that require their services. People are drawn to them because of their caring and helpful personality, which makes it easy for them to engage large groups of people. This can also allow the helper to get what they want from the groups, such as completing tasks or receiving additional assistance from others (Cloete, n.d.).

However, type two personalities frequently feel uneasy when they are alone. This occurs for a variety of reasons, one of which is that they believe they are not doing everything possible to assist someone. As a result, many professionals agree that helpers will use their personalities to mask their uncomfortable feelings. The busier they are, the less likely it is that they will be able to feel what they do not want to feel (Cloete, n.d.).

Privilege in the Self-Preservation Category

This is the opposite of type two. They are frequently misidentified as having a type seven personality. Because of their helpful nature, type twos frequently make other personalities feel as if they need to be protected. As a result, type two is frequently thought to be childish and shy. They don't mind feeling protected, but they also don't want to become overly reliant on someone else. They consider their sense of self-protection to be a privilege, and they treat it with respect. Furthermore, they have a strong fear of rejection, which leads them to believe that they must protect themselves more than others would (Cloete, n.d.).

Seduction is the One-on-One Category.

Type two personalities are known for their generosity, compassion, and selflessness, but that doesn't mean they don't want to feel important to others. No matter what level a type two personality is at, whether healthy, average, or unhealthy, they still want to be shown compassion and love. As a result, when type two personalities enter into an intimate relationship, they begin to feel a strong connection. They will frequently apply the caring and loving aspects of their personality to their partner to feel these emotions back.

When the type two personality is in a close relationship, they can become very passionate. Of course, this passion has both advantages and disadvantages. One advantage is that they will begin to feel more at ease and trust their partner. One disadvantage is that they will begin to have difficulty accepting no for an answer. They may struggle to set and adhere to boundaries (Cloete, n.d.).

Relationships with People of Other Types

Type two personalities get along best with type one and type three personalities because they are typically two's wings. They do, however, get along with people of all personalities. They will, of course, struggle with some personalities more than others.

Types two and five, for example, have difficulty getting along.

While they will eventually get along, type two sees type five as a difficult personality to form relationships with ("Relationships (Type Combinations)," n.d.).

Some of these people are better off as friends or coworkers than in a romantic relationship. Type four and type two, for example, get along exceptionally well and frequently form a very warm and compassionate relationship. They do, however, make better friends than romantic partners.

Types of Wings

Type two personalities have two wings: type one and type three.

Both of these wings not only assist type two in better managing their personality but also involve challenges. In terms of positives, type one will balance out type two by having them help everyone, not just their favorite people.

Furthermore, type one assists them in establishing boundaries so that type two is not consistently taken for granted. Type one can also assist type two in improving their surroundings. When it comes to challenges, type one can cause type two to have unrealistic expectations, become overly critical of themselves for mistakes, become overly sensitive to criticism, and neglect themselves (Cloete, n.d.).

The type three personality can help type two people with their focus, self-esteem, and ability to adapt to other people and their surroundings. The difficulty that type two faces with a type three wing is the act of neglecting themselves because they become overly focused on their work and selective when it comes to helping others (Cloete, n.d.).

The Center of Attention

If you are a type two personality, you will sit beneath the heart center point and externalize your shame (Cloete, n.d.). This is frequently what drives you to be the best person you can be, which is why you are frequently regarded as helpful and supportive. In a way, you use your shame to make yourself a better person and to help others.

This gives you the impression that you are needed and liked, which makes you feel better about your shame.

Strengths of type two:

Helpful

Generous

Supportive

Relationships

Sensitive

Type two's flaws are: Dependent on Demanding

Prideful

Privileged

Personal Development

Always remember to ask people what they require.

A type two personality desires to assist others in any way possible.

As a result, they frequently forget to ask the person what kind of assistance they truly require or desire. People may refuse to accept the assistance you provide, which means you are not truly assisting them. It is critical for both others and yourself that you focus your efforts on those who truly need assistance. Do not be afraid to ask if you can assist them in any way.

People will let you know if they truly require assistance. If they say they don't need your assistance, just let them know you're available if they do. Often, simply knowing that you are available to assist them is all that is required to make them feel loved and cared for (Cloete, n.d.).

Be Aware of Your Motives

As previously stated, there are a few levels of type two personalities who expect certain things in return and begin to believe they are entitled to be treated well because of how they treat others. This is an example of poor interior motives, which you should work on if you start feeling this way. While everyone has an internal desire to receive some of the help and compassion they give to others, if you begin to believe that you deserve this compassion and love because of your actions, you should take a step back and reconsider your motivations. You want to help others because it's in your nature to do so. You want to be compassionate to others because you have a unique personality that values compassion. You want to use these important aspects of your personality to help others rather than harm them (Cloete, n.d.).

Remember to Take Care of Yourself

You may believe that you deserve rewards because you fail to take care of yourself. This is frequently a weakness for people with type two personalities. Whatever personality you have, it is critical to make time for yourself and provide yourself with the care you require to live a happy and healthy life.

Because they are so focused on taking care of others, type two personalities frequently forget to take care of themselves. However, this can be detrimental in the long run. As a result, just as you would for anyone else, it is critical to make time for self-care and pampering. This will make it easier for you to spread your unconditional love to others (Cloete, n.d.).

CHAPTER 4

The Winner

The stress line for type three personalities runs from three to nine, while the growth line runs from three to six. An achiever is defined by the words driven, adaptable, image-conscious, and excelling. O.J. Simpson, Paul McCartney, Madonna, Muhammad Ali, Will Smith, Bill Clinton, and Michael Jordan are examples of famous achievers ("Type Three," n.d.).

What exactly is the Achiever?

Type three personalities are well known for their drive. They are regarded as workaholics who are preoccupied with what others think of them. They are known to be ambitious, energetic, diplomatic, and constantly looking for ways to advance in their lives ("Type Three," n.d.).

An achiever's greatest fear is feeling worthless both internally and externally. As a result, they will strive to be the best person they can be. They want to excel in their chosen field. Achievers also want others to notice how well they perform in their careers and other areas of their lives.

An achiever desires to feel worthwhile and valued. They frequently feel this way when they continue to meet their objectives and strive to do their best. People often look up to them because they are so ambitious. Because of everything they accomplish, many people believe that achievers are some of the most inspirational people.

Numerous factors help achievers define their success. They make use of their social standing in both their professional and personal lives. They use their popularity to gauge their success. At the same time, they define their success through their relationships with friends, family, and coworkers ("Type Three," n.d.).

Most achievers are popular because people want to be associated with them. Not only do they look up to them, but many other people believe that achievers can also help them achieve their life goals. The achiever is known to be the most liked of all personality types.

However, the need to succeed is not solely to meet their basic needs in life. Most people believe that unless they are successful, they will not receive attention from others. Type three, like any other personality, wants to feel needed and accepted by others.

As a result, they use their drive to succeed, believing that this is how they will acquire this feeling from others.

As a result, people with this personality type frequently lose sight of what they want in life. When they do this, they realize they are neglecting themselves because they have no idea what they truly want out of life. This can bring type three personalities to a fork in the road. While they want to continue to be successful so that others can give them what they want, they also recognize that they cannot continue to neglect themselves. As the achiever attempts to strike a balance, a slew of issues arise.

Integration Levels

Level of Health

The first level is the highest an achiever can achieve. Level one achievers are completely honest about their accomplishments, which are often astounding to many people. They work hard and always put forth their best effort in everything they do. They are also known to be very charitable, gentle, and accepting of themselves.

They've found a happy medium between showing off their accomplishments and taking care of themselves. Furthermore, they are known to be non-judgmental and want to see others succeed (Cloete, n.d.).

A level two achiever has high self-esteem and understands their worth.

However, they frequently refuse to acknowledge their worth to others for fear of appearing arrogant. At level two, achievers begin to pay attention to what other people think of them.

So they can continue to succeed and become the best version of themselves. They believe that people must see them in this light.

As a result, they don't believe in boasting about their achievements. They are known to be modest about their achievements in life. People regard level-two achievers as adaptable, charming, and generous (Cloete, n.d.).

A level three achiever is always striving to do their best for themselves and others. Because of their drive and ability to succeed, they are frequently regarded as role models. However, most level-three achievers are unaware of their true worth in both their professional and personal lives. One reason for this is that they are constantly striving to improve themselves. As a result, no matter what they do, they believe they can do it better. They are aware, however, that they are successful because they are proud of their accomplishments (Cloete, n.d.).

Level Average

At level four, achievers believe that their self-worth is determined by their life achievements. They will keep pushing themselves to do their best. When it comes to achieving their goals, achievers often forget about their own emotions and mentality. While others perceive them to be extremely successful, they never believe they are and continue to work even harder. One reason for this is that level four's fear of failure is intense. They are constantly concerned about how they failed or how they might fail, which fuels their desire to succeed (Cloete, n.d.).

At level five, an achiever begins to be concerned about how they appear to others. They frequently ask people what they think or feel about them. When they are told, they take the person's response to heart and do everything they can to improve themselves. At this level, achievers begin to lose sight of what they want, instead focusing on what others think they should do or what others want to see them accomplish.

Level five achievers begin to lose touch with reality and forget that they must first care for themselves (Cloete, n.d.).

At level six, an achiever begins to aggressively promote themselves. They spend a lot of time bragging about their achievements and observing what other people think about what they have accomplished. People at level six are also more likely to lie about their accomplishments to appear more accomplished than they are. At this level, they begin to show signs of narcissism and are thought to be very arrogant (Cloete, n.d.).

Unhealthy Concentration

At level seven, achievers' fear of being forgotten becomes so strong that they will go to any length to ensure that people do not forget about them or their accomplishments. At this point, they must ensure that people still believe they are superior. At this level, they want people to believe that they will never be as good as achievers (Cloete, n.d.).

At level eight, an achiever can become dishonest and manipulative. This is because they will begin to believe that they must conceal their mistakes at all costs. This is also when they begin to be envious of others who they believe are doing better than they are. To stay on top, they will start deceiving people into thinking they are better than everyone else (Cloete, n.d.).

Level nine is the lowest level for an achiever. Achievers at this level exhibit signs of psychopathic behavior or are considered narcissistic. Achievers at level nine will go to any length to ensure that they are the best and that others believe they are the best, even if it means hurting someone in the process.

Achievers at level nine will ruin someone else's happiness to get what they want and achieve their goals, or at least give the impression that they did (Cloete, n.d.).

The Achiever Social Category has subtypes.

Prestige Type three personalities are very conscious of their physical appearance. They are sometimes so concerned that they will cheat and lie to appear more successful than they are. They are competitive by nature and will go to any length to gain attention. They are also very talented, and while they can be competitive, they also work well in groups. Indeed, they are known to adapt to their social environments, which is one of the reasons they are successful (Cloete, n.d.).

The category of self-preservation is Security

The achiever's polar opposite is security. While they like to know what other people think of them and frequently base their success on their outward appearance, they don't want people to think they care what other people think of them. In some ways, achievers prefer to keep this a secret (Cloete, n.d.).

The One-on-One Category Charisma

Achievers compete for attention, but they can also be very rational about the attention they receive. Part of this is due to their security and the fact that they do not want to be in the spotlight. Another reason for this is that when achievers reach a healthy level of integration, they recognize that people don't need to be aware of all of their accomplishments.

Achievers are also known to maintain positive relationships. Many people believe that type three personalities are very supportive because they want to see others succeed.

This is especially true when high achievers collaborate. Achievers frequently believe that if they hang out with successful people, they will become successful as well (Cloete, n.d.).

Relationships with People of Other Types

The level of development of the achiever will determine how well type three gets along with other personalities. A type three with a level seven to nine personality will struggle to get along with many other people because they have high narcissistic tendencies and believe they are better than everyone else. Achievers who are more healthy or average will, on the other hand, be able to get along with almost any other personality type. The personality type that most achievers will find difficult is type six. They can, however, work well together ("Relationships (Type Combinations)," n.d.).

Types of Wings

Personality types two and four are the achiever's wings. In terms of type two, the achiever gains several advantages, such as learning how to balance work and personal life. Furthermore, type two personality assists type three in realizing that they cannot use people and must value their thoughts and beliefs. Achievers with type two can strengthen their relationships, whether they are intimate or not. Type three, on the other hand, faces unique challenges. One of these challenges is that type two can cause achievers to strive for other people's approval. This can also lead to burnout because achievers work too hard to impress others and become very critical of themselves when they believe others do not value their accomplishments (Cloete, n.d.).

Type four teaches achievers to value other people's friendships.

They assist type three in realizing that to truly achieve success, they must be true to themselves. At the same time, they assist type three in developing sensitivity to how others are feeling. This, however, can pose a challenge for high achievers. A type four personality can also cause achievers to withdraw from others, causing them to become moody or irritable. Furthermore, this may lead them to believe that others do not value them or their accomplishments.

When achievers begin to think in this manner, they begin to boast about their accomplishments and believe that others should be more appreciative and pay more attention to everything they have accomplished.

Another disadvantage that the type four wing can bring to a type three is forcing them to enter into relationships just to fill a void. If type three does not feel appreciated, they will work hard to feel appreciated in their intimate relationship (Cloete, n.d.).

The Center of Attention

A type three personality is associated with the heart center (Cloete, n.d.). If you have a type three personality, you will learn about yourself through the feedback of others. This is because you are frequently out of touch with your feelings, making it difficult to get a clear sense of who you are or how well you do on something. As a type three, you resent your sense of shame, which can lead you to your strengths and weaknesses. For example, you can transform your shame into success.

Strengths of type three:
Aim for success.
Enthusiastic -solving
Efficient
Type three's flaws include:
Overworked
Competitive
Driven
Impatient
You've lost touch with your emotions.
Personal Development
Take Regular Breaks

Because type three personalities are high achievers who are always thinking about what they can do next, they frequently forget to take care of themselves. This can quickly exhaust a person, leaving them emotionally, mentally, and physically exhausted.

When this occurs, they can quickly progress from level two or three to level five or six. As a result, achievers must remember to take breaks and prioritize their mental and emotional health.

While ambition and dedication to achieving your goals and becoming successful are admirable qualities, they can also have negative consequences. Some of these effects can be detrimental to your mental, emotional, and physical health ("Type Three," n.d.). You can, for example, drive yourself to exhaustion or become severely depressed if you do not take care of yourself. Working too hard or not taking enough time for yourself, you must remember that you can only truly succeed if you are fully charged and ready. You don't have to spend a long time charging; in fact, taking a short break can help you feel recharged.

Remember Your Passions

Because achievers are so concerned with what others think of them, they frequently overlook their interests. Instead, they try to show interest in factors that other people are interested in and want them to achieve, even if type three is not. While many achievers will continue to work towards this goal because they want to show others that they can, they can quickly begin to feel worthless or depressed because they are not working towards what they want to do ("Type Three," n.d.).

As a result, it is critical to ensure that what you are working towards is what you want to do, rather than what someone else wants you to do. You must be interested in your work or you will harm yourself mentally and emotionally. Instead of doing everything you can to impress others, you can start working with them. This way, even if you aren't completely invested in the task, you'll be surrounded by people who are, and by working as a team, you'll be able to succeed.

Be Truthful to Yourself

To truly succeed, you must be honest with yourself and with everyone else. Don't waste time exaggerating your achievements. Instead, be truthful with them. Tell them what you've accomplished and what you haven't. The more realistic you are about your accomplishments, the more people will regard you as a role model. People look up to those who are truthful. If they discover that you are constantly bragging about your accomplishments or lying about what you have accomplished, they will be less likely to regard you as successful and trustworthy ("Type Three," n.d.).

CHAPTER 5

The Independentist

Individualists are typically described as dramatic, expressive, temperamental, and self-absorbed. A type four personality's growth line shifts to a type one personality. The stress line shifts from a type four personality to a type two personality. Johnny Depp, Kate Winslet, Amy Winehouse, Billie Holiday, Judy Garland, Anne Frank, and Hank Williams are all famous people with type four personalities ("Type Four," n.d.).

What exactly is an individualist?

Type four personalities are known for being extremely sensitive to their surroundings. They have a strong emotional response. Most people feel emotions on a deeper level than other people. Of course, this can be problematic for type four because they can have difficulty controlling their feelings, which can become overwhelming. As a result, the individualist will need to employ specific techniques to manage the stress of their emotions.

Individualists will withdraw from society due to how overwhelming emotions can be. They usually have a small group of friends with whom they regularly see and talk, and they tend to withdraw from others. Their overwhelming emotions can also lead to feelings of self-pity, melancholy, or severe depression. Just because type four people tend to withdraw from society does not mean they want to live alone. Unfortunately, due to a lack of social interaction, they frequently begin to feel this way, which can exacerbate their depression or internal sadness. Individualists, on the other hand, are often anxious in social situations because they are concerned about their self-image. They are afraid of making a mistake that will cause others to judge them or think they are socially awkward, which will discourage them from participating in social situations ("Type Four," n.d.).

The most difficult emotional challenge for a type four is letting go of the past. They frequently feel guilty about mistakes they have made, especially if it has harmed their self-image. Furthermore, they have genuine difficulty letting go of emotions. As a result, type four personalities can retain emotions for years, if not decades.

Their primary desire is to feel important ("Type Four," n.d.). They want to know who they are in the world and how to understand themselves. When it comes to their greatest fear, which is also their strongest emotion, they are concerned about their identity and what distinguishing characteristics they possess. They want to stand out by doing something unique. As a result, they are frequently concerned about their significance and fear that they lack it.

This fear is so intense for the individualist because they are aware that they are not like other people. They believe they are unique, which leads them to believe that others do not understand them. While they recognize that they have distinct and one-of-a-kind abilities, they also believe that they are distinctively flawed.

As a result, they are more aware of their distinguishing characteristics than other people. They also take greater care of these characteristics than the majority of people. Individualists believe that their distinguishing features are some of the most important aspects of their personality ("Type Four," n.d.).

Type four personalities are often motivated when they can express their uniqueness. They also enjoy seeing the world's beauty and will frequently surround themselves with it. They are also motivated when they are allowed to take care of themselves before taking care of others.

They do, however, enjoy knowing that they are about to assist others ("Type Four," n.d.).

Individualists frequently believe that they are missing something in their lives, in addition to becoming overwhelmed by emotions.

Regrettably, they never fully comprehend what they are missing. As a result, they believe it could be a variety of factors and will frequently try different careers or change aspects of their personality to determine what is missing ("Type Four," n.d.). For example, some people may believe they do not have enough friends and will begin to become more social. Other individualists may believe that they are lacking a component of themselves, such as self-confidence, and will begin to boost their confidence.

Individualists' lack of self-esteem and poor self-image are two of the most serious issues they face. Both of these factors harm individualists in a variety of ways throughout their lives. For example, it may be the reason they become socially withdrawn, do not use their talent to its full potential, or are afraid to try something new for fear of what it will do to their self-image. As a result, they frequently compensate by creating an idealized image of themselves. They use this image to represent the person they want others to see them as. They will also use this fictitious version of themselves to become the best version of themselves possible.

Integration Levels

Level of Health

The highest level for an individualist is level one, which means they can let go of their past emotions, recognize they have a positive self-image, and can transform all of their life experiences into something special and valuable. These experiences can help them learn and grow, which is what they concentrate on when transforming. They also recognize their uniqueness and creativity and are not afraid to express themselves through art, music, or writing (Cloete, n.d.).

Individualists at level two are known to be extremely gentle, sensitive, and compassionate. They are aware that they deeply internalize feelings and use techniques to help them manage the feeling of being overwhelmed with emotion. They are satisfied with their self-image, but they believe that they can still improve. Furthermore, they are still looking for who they truly are (Cloete, n.d.).

Individualist at level three is truthful to themselves and others. They are aware of their emotions, but they frequently overcome them with humor. They are known to be not very serious people because they find humor in almost everything. Even if they believe their self-image has drawn some negativity, they understand that no one is perfect, and everyone makes mistakes. As a result, they are known for remaining true to themselves (Cloete, n.d.).

Average Level A type four people tend to use their creative abilities to cope with their strong emotions. They are also regarded as the most romantic individualists. They, like others, focus on creating a beautiful environment around them, even if it means inventing a fantasy to do so. They are known to have vivid imaginations but strive to remain true to their intense emotions (Cloete, n.d.).

Individualists at level five tend to take everything personally and have difficulty distinguishing between what is and isn't directed at them; as a result, they are perceived as self-absorbed, but in reality, they are hypersensitive. They are also very self-conscious and shy, making it difficult for them to be spontaneous. They are thought to be introverted. They frequently avoid social situations because it helps them protect their self-image. Another reason they are introverted is that it allows them to better control their emotions because they can express them (Cloete, n.d.).

Type four at level six tends to be more self-pitying because they realize they are different and cannot live the same way as other people. As a result, they frequently create a happier and healthier fantasy world. Others may regard a level six as self-indulgent and unproductive. At the same time, they are regarded as visionaries and unique individuals (Cloete, n.d.).

Unhealthy Concentration

Level seven is one of the unhealthy levels for a type four. At this point, Individualists have a tendency to be very angry with themselves, which causes them to withdraw socially As a result, they frequently suffer from depression Furthermore, they begin to feel embarrassed by their overwhelming emotions, causing them to block out their emotions. A level seven will frequently struggle with day-to-day functioning because they are frequently exhausted Individualists will begin to emerge.

This level occurs when their fantasy world fails and they are no longer able to imagine a brighter future for themselves (Cloete, n.d.).

A level eight person is frequently tormented by their self-image. These

Individualists typically have low self-esteem and frequently blame others for their difficulties Individualists at this level tend to despise themselves and contemplate melancholy they frequently push anyone away. Who tries to help them for a variety of reasons, including a desire to be helpful alone or believing they do not deserve assistance (Cloete, n.d.).

Individualists can reach the highest level, level nine. Type Four personalities who reach this level frequently struggle with

They use drugs and alcohol to cope with their morbid thoughts as well as low self-esteem

They frequently find themselves thinking

Suicide and various mental illnesses such as narcissism as well as avoidant personality disorders (Cloete, n.d.).

Individualist Type Subtypes

Shame is a social category.

Shame is the most fundamental emotion for a type four personality. Therefore,

This emotion is constantly present in their daily lives. They can, in fact, quickly make themselves feel guilty, causing them to also feel humiliated while they are not competitive, they do enjoy meeting new people telling them they have a positive influence on others in society

They want to know their worth because it helps them understand who they are.

They certainly are. When it comes to people, they are socially open.

People admire and support them because of the shame they feel individualists. This frequently boosts type four's confidence because they are prone to doubting their abilities

Cloete (n.d.)

Tenacity is the Self-Preservation Category.

Tenacity is the antithesis of individualism and frequently leads to failure.

They are mistaken for a type one or type seven personality. Type four personalities learn to live with their suffering through self-preservation. with some finding ways around it In fact, they frequently believe

Their suffering has made them stronger and more capable manage a variety of life circumstances As a result, they frequently look for others who they believe are suffering in the same way they are. have so that they can serve as a support system for them (Cloete, n.d.).

Competition exists in the One-on-One Category.

When it comes to sports, type four personalities are not competitive.

When there are demands, their competitive nature emerges want to be noticed by others to prove their worth. When it comes to other people believing in them, they become competitive.

They are people who are helpful, sensitive, compassionate, and generous.

Individualists can also be demanding when it comes to wishing for people to pay attention to their emotions Individualists, in some ways want people to understand what they require and value the difficulties they face as sensitive people (Cloete, n.d.).

Relationships with People of Other Types

Individualists will behave differently depending on their level of integration. influence how well they get along with others of their type If they are present at the

They have the highest level of integration and can get along with nearly everyone. other people's personalities, however, when they are below the national average and

They are less likely to have a healthy relationship if they are at an unhealthy level with other types ("Relationships (Type Combinations)," n.d.).

Types of Wings

Type three is one of the wings for type four personalities.

The benefits that achievers bring to individualists are beneficial.

Because of their type three personalities, they can express their creative fantasies.

Type four personalities can balance their internal drama so that

They can become more social, and once they do, they will be more social the setting, achievers will assist in expressing their distinct selves in a way that can entice others; additionally, type three will assist the

Type four people positively transform their life experiences.

Individualists' feelings are influenced by the challenges that their achievements bring. of having to conceal and internalize their emotions to function

Achievers can also increase the feeling of sadness that they experience.

Individualists under pressure have type four personalities will feel motivated to achieve a certain level of success (Cloete, n.d.).

The type five wing is the second wing for individualists.

It is teaching individualists to take advantage of the benefits that type five provides.

They also help them control their emotions and take things less personally and make them feel less disconnected from the world; additionally, they can assist them in thinking logically and observing society objectively

Individualists' difficulties with type 5 are exaggerated.

Their negative self-image, difficulty connecting with other people, and withdrawal from society to hide their emotions more easily (Cloete, n.d.).

Points of Interest

Individualists belong to the heart center; if you are a type four, you are an individualist personality, you want to know what makes you unique from others people (Cloete, n.d.). You are proud of your uniqueness be a strength and a weakness in your character

Furthermore, type fours tend to internalize their shame.

This is frequently how they begin to develop their distinct personality.

Strengths of type four:
Compassion
Deep emotion
Empathy
Creative
Idealistic
Type four's flaws include:
Extremely sensitive
Dissatisfaction
Demanding
Self-absorbed
Withdrawn
Moody
Personal Development
Maintain a Positive Attitude

Keeping your thoughts positive will assist you in remaining in the right frame of mind and refrain from having lengthy negative conversations with your imagination.

When you achieve this, you will notice an increase in your self-esteem and confidence, you will discover that you are capable of transforming negative life experiences into more positive ones, which will assist you in growing and learning as an individualist

One fact about having a type four personality is that you may

You will never feel as if you have found your true place in the world.

Whether you admit it to yourself or not, you frequently believe that you are unique and possess unique characteristics not shared by many others

When you begin to feel this way, remember to keep a positive attitude mindset. You must recognize that the best thing you can do is to remain calm unique, but don't isolate yourself too much from society

Cloete (n.d.)

Use Self-Control to Help You Manage Your Emotions when you practice self-discipline in your daily life, you will discover that you begin to feel less stressed and more capable of managing your emotions.

It is critical to understand that self-discipline can manifest itself in a variety of ways many forms, ranging from adhering to a daily schedule to ensuring you take

It's time to meditate or find another way to let go of your negative emotions.

For example, you will want to get enough sleep so that you can function properly better able to manage your emotions and the difficulties that come with being highly intelligent sensitive and individualistic, as well as ensuring that you find

Taking time for yourself to release any negativity will assist you in gaining improved control over transforming negative thoughts into positive ones

(Cloete, n.d.). (Cloete, n.d.).

Procrastinate not.

Another useful way to develop your personality is to avoid procrastination.

You will learn some of this through self-discipline, while others will be taught to you.

Individualists frequently put off learning until they stop procrastinating tasks until they feel ready to do them, which occurs because believe they must prepare themselves to face what

They must complete their tasks, but there is no such thing as a perfect time to do everything, especially if you don't want to do it you're doing

Procrastination can amplify your emotions, especially when it comes to working.

When it comes to negative emotions, such as stress,

Stop procrastinating and begin working on your tasks as soon as possible.

You will discover that you are more capable of dealing with your emotions.

Furthermore, you will begin to believe in yourself and your abilities.

Overall, your self-image is more positive; however, procrastination can interfere.

With a positive attitude, you want to do everything you can to help complete your assignments as soon as possible (Cloete, n.d.).

CHAPTER 6

The Detective

The investigator's growth line extends from point 5 to point 8, while its stress line extends from point 5 to point 7. The investigator, who is also known as the observer and the specialist, is described as innovative, isolated, perceptive, and secretive. Siddhartha Gautama Buddha, Stephen Hawking, Vincent van Gogh, Tim Burton, and Kurt Cobain are some well-known investigators ("Type Five," n.d.).

What exactly is the Investigator?

A type five personality's greatest desire is to be knowledgeable and skilled. An investigator's greatest fear is being perceived as ineffective and incapable. Investigators can focus on very detailed and complicated tasks and are generally insightful. They are also very curious and easily distracted by their thoughts and the situations around them. Learning, being able to defend themselves from society with their knowledge, and understanding the environment and people around them are the most important motivators for a type five personality ("Type Five," n.d.).

Investigators are the type of people who want to know the truth.

They want to learn the truth, but they also want to know the detailed version of the truth. They want to know every detail, including why something occurred, when it occurred, and how it occurred.

Unfortunately, this can lead investigators to believe that they will never be able to fully function in today's society. They may become more withdrawn as a result of their fear of what will happen ("Type Five," n.d.).

Of course, this feeling is exacerbated because type five personalities believe they are incapable of completing tasks that others can. They lack the strong self-confidence that most other personalities have, which can often prevent them from becoming successful.

To fully comprehend why something is happening, investigators must be able to observe it. They will then take the time necessary to comprehend what they saw, and heard, and why it occurred.

They are critical thinkers who will take the time necessary to reach a decision. Of course, this can cause problems when it comes to meeting deadlines and communicating with others. This frequently leads to the misconception that investigators procrastinate. They do not, however, procrastinate as much as most other personalities. Instead, they're simply taking their time to figure out what happened and come to their conclusions ("Type Five," n.d.).

Type five personalities are constantly creating and inventing new things as a result of their observation and critical thinking abilities. They can take something apart, put it back together, or create something new because they want to see how things work. These abilities instill confidence in investigators as they begin to believe they can carve out their niche in the world. At the same time, their need to observe, learn, and create causes them to withdraw from society. While they are content with a small circle of friends, they often feel lonely ("Type Five," n.d.).

One of the most difficult challenges for investigators is that they dislike confronting their problems. As a result, they frequently struggle to form relationships and, in general, to function in society, particularly within groups of people. Having to complete a task as part of a team is one of the most difficult challenges that investigators can face. They perform tasks much better on their own ("Type Five," n.d.).

Integration Levels

Levels of Health

Level one is the healthiest level for an investigator. Individuals of type five who reach this level are open-minded. They are also pioneer investigators. They frequently spend their time devising new ways to complete tasks.

Level two can gain a lot of insight from everything they encounter in life. They have a strong ability to concentrate on tasks, but they can become too engrossed in the task, causing them to lose sight of what they needed to do in the first place. Because of their observational skills, they are very observant, mentally alert, and good at predicting what will happen in the future (Cloete, n.d.).

A level three is always looking for new things to learn. They frequently become experts in their field of study, are self-sufficient, and skilled masters (Cloete, n.d.).

Levels on the Average

A level four investigator will frequently try to find new ways to do something. They will perceive things as a challenge, which will aid in their ability to absorb the information they seek. They are frequently preoccupied with gathering as many resources as possible to expand their knowledge. Around this level, the investigator begins to become aware of their abilities and works on ways to improve them (Cloete, n.d.).

A level five will begin to succumb to their fantasy world. While they remain curious and continue to broaden their knowledge, they become detached from what they learn and the ideas that knowledge instills in them. During this stage, they begin to focus on darker topics, which can contribute to their increasingly morbid thoughts as they become trapped within their minds (Cloete, n.d.).

A level six investigator is considered argumentative and pessimistic.

While they continue to learn, they do not focus on expanding their knowledge as much as investigators at healthy or higher average levels do. A type five personality prefers to be alone with their thoughts and tends to withdraw from society (Cloete, n.d.).

Unhealthy Concentrations

A level seven investigator is both aggressive and unstable.

They are victims of their dark thoughts, which frequently cause them to be repulsed by others. As a result, they become increasingly socially isolated (Cloete, n.d.).

An investigator on level eight becomes horrified by their increasingly dark thoughts. As they continue to delve into these thoughts, they become terrified of them and frequently realize that they are unhealthy. However, most people try not to think about how horrifying their thoughts are as they become increasingly obsessed with them (Cloete, n.d.).

Level nine is the most dangerous level for an investigator. A type five personality will frequently experience a psychotic break at this point. They are frequently diagnosed with mental disorders such as schizophrenia (Cloete, n.d.).

The Investigator's Subtypes

Social Classification is Totem

One of the reasons a type five personality is known as the investigator is that they frequently exhibit characteristics associated with investigators.

People with this personality type are drawn to the details of their surroundings. They want to know why and how something happened. To figure out what is going on, they will frequently conduct their research or speak with others. They don't tend to listen to what others have to say, partly because they are known to disconnect from others. By disconnecting, they can better manage their emotions and thoughts, which can help them learn with a clear mind (Cloete, n.d.).

Castle is in the Self-Preservation Category.

Because they tend to withdraw from society, investigators are thought to be introverts. They maintain close relationships with a small group of friends and prefer to stay at home to maintain clear social boundaries. At the same time, they are frequently seen observing people and situations in an attempt to determine what is going on around them and why. Their desire to be left alone in their home can often have a negative impact because they may become overly protective of their privacy, making it difficult for them to relax their guard if they require assistance or if others wish to socialize with them (Cloete, n.d.).

One-on-One classification is Confident

Investigators will develop strong feelings of compassion and passion for a couple of people in their personal lives. However, this can either help them thrive socially or cause them to put their partner or friends to the test to ensure that they will not be harmed or betrayed by them. A type five personality may put their partner to the test because they are afraid of letting down their guard. At the same time, investigators may overprotect their partner because they do not want to share this person with anyone else (Cloete, n.d.).

Relationships with People of Other Types

Investigators, like the other types of personalities, can get along with anyone. They are, however, more compatible with type three personalities and less compatible with type two personalities. Any personality that a type five meets can either help them thrive or cause them to struggle even more. However, because type five is typically non-confrontational, they will rarely express their emotions.

They will instead begin to withdraw from people and society as a whole ("Relationships (Type Combinations)," n.d.).

Types of Wings

Type four, also known as the individualist, is one of the investigator's wing types. Type four can assist type five in finding balance in their lives, particularly when it comes to how passionate they become about certain people. Connecting with others, learning how to connect their emotions to their thoughts, and connecting themselves to their intuitions are all strengths. The difficulties that this wing type presents to the investigator include becoming attached to fantasies, becoming depressed because they feel misunderstood by society, and withdrawing further from society to avoid confrontation (Cloete, n.d.).

A type six personality is the investigator's second wing type.

Type six strengths include the ability to understand someone else's point of view, increasing their connection with groups of people, and increasing their self-confidence so they are more comfortable in social settings. The differences between type five and type six are that type five may become more socially withdrawn because they believe they can't trust people and that being overly social will upset people (Cloete, n.d.).

Points of Interest

You are a member of the head center if you have a type five personality (Cloete, n.d.). You believe that you must know everything about the situation before entering it. As a result, you will frequently observe everything that is going on so that you know exactly what to expect.

Strengths of Type 5:

Intellectual
Self-reliant
Calm
Thoughtful Type five's flaws include:
Overthinking
Hoarding
Isolation
Personal Development

Learn to Unwind

Investigators frequently struggle with learning to unwind. This can cause them to become more intense, causing them to withdraw from people because they don't want to cause any problems, especially since they dislike confrontation. As a result, type five personalities must take extra precautions to ensure that they can unwind and find something, such as a hobby, that will help them relieve some of the stressors in their lives. Going for a walk, riding a bike, or joining a gym, for example, are all excellent ways to relieve stress. However, because some investigators are highly creative, they may be able to relieve their stress through art or writing (Cloete, n.d.).

Distractions should be avoided.

Type five personalities are inquisitive about everything, which can lead to distraction. When this happens, they frequently forget about the tasks they need to complete or fall behind on them, necessitating a deadline extension or pushing the work aside. As a result, it is critical to complete your tasks, even if it means exercising self-discipline or discovering techniques to help you avoid becoming distracted by situations that aren't as important (Cloete, n.d.).

Don't Allow Your Thoughts to Trap You

Investigators can easily become trapped in their thoughts because they are constantly thinking and trying to learn new things. When this occurs, they tend to avoid the people around them and withdraw even further from society. Because this can cause an investigator to become lonely over time, often leading to depression, they must schedule social time into their calendar. Even if you only have a few friends, which many personalities are fine with, you will want to make time to go to the movies, eat out, or hang out with them at home and play video games. This will help you maintain a sense of balance in your life and avoid feeling trapped by your thoughts (Cloete, n.d.).

CHAPTER 7

The Loyalist Party

Line three is the stress line for the sixth personality type, the loyalist. The growth line extends from point 6 to point 9. A loyalist is defined by the words responsible, suspicious, engaging, and anxious. Prince Harry and Mel Gibson are two famous people who have loyalist personalities. "Type Six," n.d., stars Mark Wahlberg, Julia Roberts, Mark Twain, Malcolm X, and Robert F. Kennedy.

What exactly is a Loyalist?

Type six personalities are known to be excellent problem solvers. They are typically capable of problem-solving quickly and are regarded as hardworking, reliant, and trustworthy.

Some of their motivations include receiving support from others, feeling secure, and being able to overcome their fears and anxiety. Because loyalists can often predict the future, they become defensive and wary of situations that could result in unfavorable outcomes ("Type Six," n.d.).

A loyalist's fundamental desire is to feel safe and supported by those around them. A loyalist's greatest fear is losing the guidance and support of those closest to them.

They are known to be the most loyal to their close friends and family of all nine personality types in the Enneagram theory. They can become just as devoted to their ideas and beliefs.

They can, however, become withdrawn, and aggressive, and show signs of paranoia if they reach an unhealthy level ("Type Six," n.d.).

One disadvantage of a type six personality is a lack of self-confidence. This is why they frequently seek advice and approval from others. They believe they are incapable of performing tasks that others can. If they cannot find someone to guide them to a healthy balance, they will guide themselves using their imagination and what they believe is right ("Type Six," n.d.).

Loyalists are members of the thinking center, which means they are always thinking. They are also easily terrified of their thoughts. This is frequently due to an internal fear that they will be incorrect and cause problems for others. This explains why they have high levels of anxiety.

The anxiety that a loyalist feels frequently leads to an unhealthy level of integration. Loyalists are often aware of their anxiety, so they do everything they can to combat it ("Type Six," n.d.). They are more likely to follow a healthy level of integration if they are successful. If they are not successful, they are more likely to succumb to an unhealthy level of integration.

Because their anxiety is so strong, they frequently spend time looking for the sources of their anxiety. They will eventually realize there is no reason for their anxious behavior over something trivial.

The most difficult challenge for a type six personality is attempting to build a safety net to maintain a healthy level of integration ("Type Six," n.d.). They also want to create this sense of security to protect themselves from their anxiety, thoughts, and emotions. They believe that if they can create a safety net, they will be able to deal with life's stresses.

Integration Levels

Level of Health

Loyalists at the healthiest level, i.e. level one, are among the most optimistic thinkers. They are known to be independent and have complete faith in their feelings and beliefs. They are brave, trusting of others, and believe in true equality (Cloete, n.d.).

A loyalist at level two believes that trust is essential and that most people can be trusted. They are known to have strong bonds with others and to feel deeply (Cloete, n.d.).

A level three loyalist is hardworking, trustworthy, responsible, and has a strong sense of community involvement.

They frequently devote themselves to social movements in which they strongly believe. They believe that the world can be made safe for everyone and are willing to make sacrifices to make this happen (Cloete, n.d.).

Average a level four loyalist appreciates schedules, organization, and structure. They will spend the majority of their time attempting to improve environmental conditions for others, but they will not always think through their actions. Their primary goal is to keep everything and everyone safe (Cloete, n.d.).

When they believe that people are taking advantage of them or asking them to take on too much, a level five loyalist will become passive-aggressive. They have internal confusion about how to better themselves, as well as negative thought patterns that can cause them to become angry and annoyed with others (Cloete, n.d.).

A loyalist at level six will frequently blame others for their problems and become very insecure about who they are.

They are distrustful of others because they believe that people cannot be trusted. They have a reputation for being sarcastic, defensive, and argumentative. As a result, many loyalists retreat from society (Cloete, n.d.).

Unhealthy Concentration

A level seven loyalist will become extremely unstable and defenseless. They will seek out an authoritative figure who can teach them how to defend themselves, and once found, they will become extremely reliant on this authoritative figure. However, they frequently struggle with relationships, which drives them even further into isolation. Loyalists at this level may feel increasingly isolated (Cloete, n.d.).

Loyalists at level eight tend to become paranoid.

They believe that everyone is out to get them and that no one can be trusted.

When they are afraid, they frequently resort to violence (Cloete, n.d.).

A loyalist at level nine is frequently diagnosed with an avoidant personality disorder or paranoid personality disorder. They frequently consider suicide as a means of escaping their paranoid and self-destructive thoughts (Cloete, n.d.).

Duty is a subtype of the Loyalist Social Category.

This subcategory's type six personalities are frequently compared to type one personalities. This is because they both have similar characteristics. Loyalists will do everything in their power to assist those they believe are weaker than them. They are also very strict about following rules and guidelines. They are known to be hard workers who will go to any length to ensure that the tasks assigned to them are completed successfully (Cloete, n.d.).

Warmth is the Self-Preservation Category.

Loyalists are frequently afraid of making a mistake, which is why they do not share their thoughts or opinions. They are known to be caring and warm people who get along with people of all personalities.

They frequently spend their time with others because they enjoy their company. At the same time, they may be concerned about others noticing their insecurities (Cloete, n.d.).

Intimidation is the One-on-One Category.

This subtype is the polar opposite of the loyalist. They are frequently bold and are not afraid to take the necessary steps to defend themselves. They are known to be emotionally and mentally strong individuals who, no matter how terrified they are, may run toward danger rather than away from it. This subtype of loyalists may be perceived as intimidating (Cloete, n.d.).

Relationships with People of Other Types

Type six personalities make excellent friends and partners for people of all personality types. While they tend to become fast friends with personalities nine, two, three, and four, they can still have disagreements with these individuals. Of course, a type six personality can get along with another type six personality. They will, however, frequently try to avoid confrontation because they share many of the same characteristics ("Relationships (Type Combinations)," n.d.).

Types of Wings

A type five personality is one wing type for the loyalist. The investigator's strengths include allowing the loyalist to be more accepting of other points of view, keeping their fears in check through analysis, allowing them to trust their internal validations, and feeling more confident in themselves. The difficulties that loyalists face with investigators include increasing their anxiety and avoiding confrontation (Cloete, n.d.).

A type seven personality is another wing type for the loyalist. The qualities that this personality brings to the loyalist include trusting others, being optimistic, and feeling at ease in society.

The weaknesses that type seven brings to a type six personality include ideas on how to avoid confrontation and fear of pain, as well as anxiety over trivial matters (Cloete, n.d.).

Points of Interest

If you have a type six personality, you are part of the head center and are more likely to imagine the worst-case scenario when confronted with danger (Cloete, n.d.). This is your natural reaction to danger because you believe it will assist you in preparing for what may occur. While you generally seek guidance from authoritative figures, you will rebel against them because you believe they become too attached to you and you want more independence from them.

Strengths of type six:

Critical-thinking
Strategizing
Bravery
Sensitivity
Humor
Loyalty
Type six's flaws include:
Excessive vigor
Anxiety
Pessimism
Hyper-vigilant

How to Grow Personally Recognize That Anxiety Is Normal

Many people around the world suffer from anxiety. Anxiety is present in all nine Enneagram personality types. When a loyalist remembers that their anxiety does not distinguish them from the other personality types, they are better able to deal with life's stresses. Loyalists frequently believe that they are the only ones who experience anxiety, even though everyone experiences different types of anxiety. Some people are anxious about insignificant situations and thoughts. Everyone experiences worry daily. Furthermore, everyone can learn techniques to help them deal with their insecurities and anxious thoughts (Cloete, n.d.).

Anxiety and stress go hand in hand. As a result, once you've identified your stressors, you'll be able to learn how to manage them effectively. You learn to manage your anxiety and anxious thoughts (Cloete, n.d.).

Improve Your Self-Confidence and Trustworthiness

When a loyalist is in good health, they are trusting and self-confident. Every loyalist can reach this level, and one way to do so is to learn to trust others. Type six personalities must learn to trust that others think they are generally nice people.

They must believe in themselves that people do not think negatively of them and that this is all part of their anxiety and anxious thinking. If they can change their mindset, they will become more trusting and self-confident (Cloete, n.d.).

CHAPTER 8

The Passionate

The enthusiast's stress line runs from point seven to point two, while the growth line runs from point seven to point five. A type eight personality is defined by the words acquisitive, spontaneous, scattered, and versatile. Famous enthusiasts include Thomas Jefferson, Amelia Earhart, Robert Downey, Jr., Charlie Sheen, Paris Hilton, and Larry King ("Type Seven," n.d.).

What exactly is the Enthusiast?

Freedom, keeping themselves occupied, being happy, and avoiding pain are some of the main motivators for the enthusiast. Their main fear is being in pain, and their main desire is to know that their needs are met. Type seven personalities are known to be high-spirited, playful, gifted, optimistic, and disorganized. While they are always looking for new and exciting adventures, they can also become easily exhausted from their adventures ("Type Seven," n.d.).

They are extremely curious about life and have big, exciting eyes when they look around. In fact, many people compare them to a child in a candy store. While they are upbeat, they can also be dominant ("Type Seven," n.d.).

While they are at the head or thinking center, this does not necessarily imply that they consider all options before making a decision. They can, in fact, be very impulsive. They can concentrate on their thoughts while also being very practical. Indeed, some people believe that enthusiasts have two personalities that they can switch between in an instant ("Type Seven," n.d.). For example, they can transition from being very playful and impulsive to acting and speaking maturely and thoughtfully.

Type seven personalities enjoy learning and will frequently spend their time seeking out new information to absorb. As a result, they are known for being quick learners. As a result, they are able to learn new skills ("Type Seven," n.d.). They place a high value on their abilities, which can lead to conflict as they try to figure out what career path to take in their lives.

Enthusiasts are frequently disconnected from their thinking center, which causes them to be impulsive ("Type Seven," n.d.). This can also cause issues for those attempting to guide them in a healthy direction of integration. In turn, a type seven personality may experience anxiety. When they begin to feel anxious, they will distract themselves from something. At the same time, they can have difficulty making the right decisions.

Integration Levels

Level of Health

Level-one enthusiasts are frequently in awe of their surroundings. They are extremely grateful for what they have and believe that everyone acts with the best of intentions. They believe that people want to work together to improve the world. They also believe that we are making progress in this effort (Cloete, n.d.).

A level two enthusiast is an extrovert who is very spontaneous. They, like the first level, believe that people have a common good and are very optimistic about the future. They believe that if we continue to collaborate, we will make the world a

When trying to do the best for others, a level three enthusiast focuses on specific areas of their community. They are known to be high achievers and are very realistic about their goals (Cloete, n.d.).

Level Average

A level four enthusiast is more concerned with money and trends than with making the world a better place. They are dissatisfied with the options presented to them by life and frequently seek out new experiences (Cloete, n.d.).

A level five enthusiast is afraid of becoming bored with tasks and people. As a result, they are known to be outgoing and loud. Furthermore, they are known to be hyperactive.

They are excellent performers. Furthermore, they frequently struggle to determine what they require and desire (Cloete, n.d.).

A level six enthusiast is very materialistic, greedy, and self-centered. This can make them very demanding because they frequently believe they never have enough. The more money they make, for example, the more money they want to receive the next time. They are never truly thankful for what they have (Cloete, n.d.).

Unhealthy Concentration

A level seven enthusiast can become abusive and aggressive. They are frequently addicted to drugs and alcohol and have difficulty knowing when to stop, particularly when they know they want something. They have a lot of money problems because they don't know how to manage their money (Cloete, n.d.).

An enthusiast at level eight is unable to control their impulses. Their anxiety can reach new heights at this point as they realize they can't control themselves. They also begin to act out as a result of their impulses and frustrations when they are unable to obtain what they desire (Cloete, n.d.).

A level nine enthusiast is frequently diagnosed with bipolar disorder because they experience severe highs and severe lows. They are having difficulty coping because they realize they are unable to manage their stresses and impulses. Many enthusiasts often begin to consider suicide at this point (Cloete, n.d.).

Sacrifice is a subtype of the Enthusiast Social Category.

The sacrifice is the enthusiast's polar opposite. This subtype frequently sacrifices their own needs in order to make the world a better place, particularly for those they love and support. At the same time, they want to be recognized for their sacrifices, which causes them to be judgmental of others if their efforts are not recognized (Cloete, n.d.).

The network is in the Self-Preservation Category.

A type seven personality is considered extroverted because they enjoy socializing with others, particularly their close friends and family. They know how to help others and are frequently willing to do so, especially if it means more fun for their group. However, they may become overly involved in pleasing others, as this can become a motivator for them, sending them into an unhealthy level of integration (Cloete, n.d.).

Fascination is the one-on-one category.

Enthusiasts are known for their optimism and eagerness, which is how they got their name. However, they can become so preoccupied with the fantasy of making the world a better place that they lose sight of reality. When they see how the world really is, they begin to see it as a grey place. This frequently leads them to believe that the people with whom they associate are dull and unwilling to assist them in making the world a more colorful and happier place (Cloete, n.d.).

Relationships with People of Other Types

A type seven personality can get along with any other personality type, but they prefer to associate with types two, three, seven, and nine. In fact, they get along best with people of type nine. Of course, as with any personality type, these relationships bring both strengths and weaknesses ("Relationships (Type Combinations)," n.d.).

Types of Wings

A type six personality, also known as the loyalist, is one of the wing types for a type seven personality. The loyalist, like any other wing, can bring both strengths and challenges to their relationship. Commitment and a deeper understanding of their actions, mindfulness, and the act of taking things more seriously are some of the strengths that a type six can bring to the lives of type seven. Exaggeration of fears, feeling like responsibilities are a burden, self-doubt, and the feeling of being irresponsible are some of the challenges that the loyalist brings to the enthusiast (Cloete, n.d.).

A type eight personality is the enthusiast's second wing type.

Assertiveness, learning to plan better, becoming less afraid of feeling hurt, and learning to be honest with themselves and others are some of the strengths that type eight brings.

The difficulties that type eight presents to an enthusiast include turning assertiveness into aggression, seeking immediate gratification, and becoming self-absorbed (Cloete, n.d.).

Types of Centers

If you have a type seven personality, you belong to the head center and will try to make your uncomfortable, fearful situations more exciting and comfortable (Cloete, n.d.). This happens because people with type seven are afraid of becoming trapped in fearful situations. As a result, they will do whatever they can to reduce their fear.

Strengths of type seven:

Energetic
Quick-thinker
 Vivid imagination
Playful
Type seven's flaws include:
Impatient
Self-absorbed
Unrealistic
Isolation
Uncommitted

How to Develop Personally

Control Your Emotions

You will be able to make better decisions and realize that you cannot have everything exactly the way you want it and when you want it once you learn to control your impulses. When you reach this realization, you will be able to determine whether you truly require something or merely desire something. Furthermore, you will gain a better understanding of what is and is not good for you (Cloete, n.d.).

Pay Attention to Others

When you begin to listen to other people, you will begin to learn more than you ever imagined possible. You will begin to make better decisions because you will believe that others want the best for you and will not lead you astray. You will also discover that other people can be very interesting and can assist you in becoming a better person. Furthermore, you will learn to appreciate your alone time because the more you interact with others, the more you will realize that you require solitude to remain relaxed (Cloete, n.d.).

CHAPTER 9

The Defender

The protector, also known as the controller, is a type eight personality. This is because, while they care about the environment, they also want to maintain control over everything and everyone around them. The challenger is another name for the protector. The protector's stress line runs from point eight to point five, and the growth line runs from point eight to point two. Decisive, confrontational, self-confident, and willful are some of the most common terms used to describe the type eight personality.

Some of the most well-known protectors include John Wayne, Bette Davis, Roseanne Barr, Aretha Franklin, and Martin Luther King, Jr. ("Type Eight," n.d.).

What exactly is the Protector?

The protector is known for being powerful, self-assured, protective, resourceful, and assertive. They can also become domineering and feel the need to control everything around them at the same time.

A type's main desire is to be able to protect itself. Their greatest fear is being controlled by others or being harmed by someone. They want to be able to protect themselves in the same way that they want to protect their environment and others ("Type Eight," n.d.).

Some of the main motivations for type eight personalities include the ability to resist their weaknesses, demonstrate their strengths, control their environment, and become self-reliant (Type Eight, "n.d.).

One of the main reasons why the protector is also known as the challenger is that this personality type is the most likely to challenge themselves and others ("Type Eight," n.d.). In fact, they like to see how far they can go and, as a result, gain confidence when they see themselves succeeding in tasks they consider difficult.

Because they must exert control over their surroundings, type eight personalities are often referred to as protectors. While some may perceive this as domineering, type eight personalities do it to protect everything around them, including themselves and others. Protectors desire complete control over the environment in order to protect everyone, including themselves ("Type Eight," n.d.).

The most common fear of type eight is harm; however, there is another aspect to this fear. This includes not only harm to themselves, but also harm to others and their environment. Protectors realize early on that they must be persistent and strong if they are to become the protectors they believe they must be.

This is because they are aware that they must do everything possible to avoid causing harm to themselves or others. As a result, while they are most concerned about harm to others and the environment, they are more concerned about a loss of control than actual harm. This is because they recognize the importance of maintaining control in order to protect themselves, others, and the environment ("Type Eight," n.d.).

Despite their fear of being harmed, they can usually withstand a great deal of physical harm. This is due to their reputation for being emotionally, mentally, and physically tough. They can, however, handle physical harm far better than emotional and mental harm. In fact, they would prefer to be physically harmed. This is because they place a high value on their health and frequently take it for granted ("Type Eight," n.d.). Of course, this can cause problems with other personalities because type eight personalities are less likely to prioritize their own health in favor of the well-being of others.

Type eight personalities are concerned with environmental issues. While the protector believes he or she is doing the right thing, others will not. This can catch the protector off guard and make him or her wonder why people think otherwise when he or she works so hard to ensure that everyone is cared for and protected. When this occurs, they tend to become emotionally distant from those closest to them. Unfortunately, when type eight feels this way, he or she will also withdraw from society ("Type Eight," n.d.). This occurs because the protector feels misunderstood and rejected, which causes emotional harm.

Integration Levels

Level of Health

Level one protectors are their own masters. They are self-controlling, courageous, and willing to put themselves in physical danger to obtain what they desire. Protectors at this level are frequently regarded as heroes because they are constantly working to protect their environment and others above themselves (Cloete, n.d.).

Level two type eight personalities are known to be very strong and self-confident. They understand what they want and need and can be very assertive when it comes time to act. They have the mindset that they can truly take over the world (Cloete, n.d.).

Level three protectors are natural-born leaders. People look up to them because they are authoritative and commanding.

They do whatever it takes to ensure that action occurs.

In general, type eight personalities are regarded as very caring, strong, protective, excellent providers, and honorable (Cloete, n.d.).

Level Average

Protectors at the fourth level have a strong desire for financial independence. They understand the resources required to achieve independence and are not afraid to take risks or work hard to achieve it. While they may appear to be protective of others, their primary goal is to obtain what they desire. They don't often ignore their own needs to help others; they ignore their own needs to achieve the financial independence they desire (Cloete, n.d.).

A level five type eight personality is concerned with dominating not only their environment but also other people. Many people begin to see this as a form of control rather than a form of protection.

This is because they have a bossy demeanor and can be quite forceful. At this level, protectors will begin to believe that people are not treating them with the respect they deserve, and thus they are not treated as equals (Cloete, n.d.).

Level six protectors are known to be extremely intimidating. People with other types of personalities, in fact, begin to be afraid of what they are capable of at this level.

In order to get what they want, they can become very confrontational and loud. They are unwilling to back down and will continue to use threats to persuade others to listen to them (Cloete, n.d.).

Unhealthy Level Protectors at level seven have one of the highest unhealthiest levels. They become completely dictatorial at this point in order to get people to listen to them and give them control.

While other personalities begin to band together against them, they will become ruthless in order to maintain their dominance. Protectors at this level have a reputation for being violent criminals and con artists (Cloete, n.d.).

Protectors at level eight frequently develop delusory beliefs about their power. They believe they are impenetrable (Cloete, n.d.).

Type eight personalities with level nine personalities are known to have sociopathic tendencies. If they feel threatened, they will destroy everything and everyone in their path. In fact, they would rather be destroyed than surrender to anyone else. Protectors at this level are barbaric and frequently exhibit antisocial personality disorder symptoms (Cloete, n.d.).

Solidarity is a subtype of the Protector Social Category.

Solidarity is viewed as the polar opposite of a type eight personality.

Protectors in this group are frequently regarded as type two rather than type eight. This is because they tend to prioritize helping others over their own needs and desires.

This subtype's protectors have a strong desire to help the world socially by focusing on social issues that they believe are important.

They despise injustice and are extremely sensitive to the needs of others. At the same time, they will act as a shield for anyone they believe is being treated unfairly (Cloete, n.d.).

Satisfaction is the Self-Preservation Category.

Many people believe that this subtype's protector has two distinct personalities. People will first notice that this person is very caring and generous. As a mother, father, aunt, uncle, or sibling, they typically have a very comforting nature and can become a guardian or role model to many people. In this role, type eight personalities will go to any length to assist those in need. They believe, however, that they should be able to get just as much in return. When they want something, they can become aggressive and manipulative, and this is when people notice a different side to this subtype. While they will ensure that everyone else's needs are met, they will also ensure that their own needs are met (Cloete, n.d.).

The One-on-One Category Possession

Type eight personalities who belong to this subtype are seen as leaders and rebels. They will go to any length to ensure that they reach the top and get to where they want to go. Because they can be very impulsive when they want something, this subtype is easily mistaken for a type four personality.

They do not, however, exhibit the characteristics of a type four personality. They act this way because they become unapologetic when they want to achieve a goal (Cloete, n.d.).

Relationships with People of Other Types

Type eight personalities, like the other personality types, tend to get along with other type eights ("Relationships (Type Combinations)," n.d.). If all of the personality types are at a healthy level of integration rather than an unhealthy level, the relationship will progress. This is not to say that the protector will not experience conflict with other personality types. A relationship with a type three personality, for example, can become too much of a good thing for the protector. They will ignore the challenges they face together because they are both very positive when they are at a healthy level of integration. This means that when they disagree, they tend to avoid confronting each other. Instead, they will keep their disagreements to themselves and continue to collaborate. As a result, they may become increasingly hostile to one another.

Center for Wings

The protector has one type seven wing. This personality type's strengths include a balance of planning and perspective, happiness, the realization that they do not have to complete tasks alone, and understanding the value of expressing their thoughts and emotions. Type eight may face challenges such as an increase in their addictive personality, the need to fulfill their desires, and becoming increasingly self-absorbed. They will also be less concerned with the consequences of their actions (Cloete, n.d.).

A type nine wing is a type eight's second wing. This wing can provide the protector with a variety of benefits and challenges. Some of the protector's strengths include the realization that he or she does not need to force something to happen if it can happen naturally, a sense of balance in life, and becoming more laid back and calm. The difficulties include neglecting oneself, losing touch with oneself, and withdrawing from society. When a protector withdraws from those around them, they feel guilty and harshly judge themselves (Cloete, n.d).

Type of Center

People with a type eight personality are not only associated with the body center but they are also known for their anger and temper issues (Cloete, n.d.). They express their rage in public and are not afraid to do so. However, they also want to protect themselves, so they will frequently construct guards as a form of defense. Most of the time, they become enraged because they believe someone is being mistreated.

Strengths of type eight:

Fairness
Generosity
Bravery
Strength
Honest \

Type eight's flaws include:

Forgetful
Controlling
Angry
Fear of displaying vulnerability
Personal Development

Use Your Authority Wisely

Making sure you use your power wisely is one of the best ways to grow personally. You have a strong sense of power and the ability to do a lot of good with it; however, in order to avoid falling victim to an unhealthy level of integration, you must know how to use it.

Unfortunately, it is natural for people who have a lot of power to believe they want more of it. However, if you act with self-control, you will realize that your power is used to help and uplift people rather than control them and the environment.

When it comes to dealing with a crisis, you are extremely helpful. When times are tough, you can use your power to keep a cool head and make people feel more at ease. This is a very unique trait to possess because you are the only person who possesses this level of power. As a result, it is critical to use your power wisely and with good intentions (Cloete, n.d.).

Maintain Control of Your Ego

Most people struggle with their ego, whether it is expressed externally or internally. As a protector, you frequently use your ego to defend yourself. As a result, as your ego grows, you will begin to believe that you need to protect yourself more from other people and environmental factors. As a result, you will become more sensitive to any slight disrespect or threat to your environment. This can lead to you acting out, sometimes violently. To maintain a healthy level of integration, you must keep your ego in check so that you do not begin to overthink perceived threats (Cloete, n.d.).

CHAPTER 10

The Arbiter

The mediator, also known as the peacemaker, is a type nine personality. This is due to the fact that their main descriptive words are agreeable, complacent, reassuring, and receptive. They are also known for being laid-back, accepting, and trusting. Their stress line extends from point 9 to point 6, and their growth line extends from point 9 to point 3. Queen Elizabeth II, John F. Kennedy, Jr., Abraham Lincoln, Janet Jackson, Jim Henson, and Walt Disney are among the most well-known mediators ("Type Nine," n.d.).

What exactly is the Mediator?

Some of the most important motivators for mediators are the ability to bring peace into their environment, resist something that could disrupt them, and avoid conflict. Their greatest desire is peace of mind, and their greatest fear is separation or loss. In a nutshell, they are known to be accepting, creative, and supportive. Indeed, one of the main reasons they are often referred to as peacemakers rather than mediators is that they are the type of person who will go to any length to bring peace into their environment and the lives of others ("Type Nine," n.d.).

Simultaneously, type nine personalities will go out of their way to ignore what is wrong in the world and with other people ("Type Nine," n.d.). They dislike confrontation, so they will use any means possible to bring peace to the situation and environment. If they are unable to bring peace to a situation, they frequently become numb.

Mediators can also lose touch with reality. When this happens, they often retreat to their minds and create a fantasy world to help them cope with whatever is going on around them, whether good or bad. This is the point at which type nine personalities begin to use their personality powers against themselves ("Type Nine," n.d.). They will feel so out of sorts that they will struggle in their daily lives.

However, if type nine personalities can maintain their balance, they will be able to use their abilities to help people in difficult situations. They will use their energy to make peace with the situation once they are aware of what they are capable of. When they reach this level, they can critically think about the best way to solve the problem peacefully rather than ignoring it ("Type Nine," n.d.). After all of this, they will begin to believe that if they are unable to resolve the entire problem, there is still a problem. As a result, mediators believe it is best to resolve the issue as soon as possible so that it does not reoccur.

Mediators are also known as one of the most spiritual Enneagram personalities. This is because they are known to be spiritual seekers who want to form strong internal connections not only with people but also with their surroundings and the universe as a whole. In fact, while they are constantly working to keep people at peace, they are also working to create harmony within the world. To truly believe they are doing their job, they must keep an open mind, focus on relaxation, let go of tension, avoid mental, emotional, and physical pain, practice patience, and believe in unity over separation ("Type Nine," n.d.).

Levels of Integration Healthy Level A mediator at a level where one feels fulfilled and at one with themselves. They are most satisfied with their lives, have excellent interpersonal relationships, and have strong ties to their surroundings (Cloete, n.d.).

Level two type nine personalities are emotionally stable and calm. They have high regard for other people and regard mediators as trustworthy. They are also known for their patience, good nature, and genuine concern for people and the environment. Many people believe they live simple, uncomplicated lives (Cloete, n.d.).

Level three mediators are extremely supportive and want the best for others. They are reassuring, optimistic, and have a calming effect on others. They are thought to be natural healers who excel at bringing people together for the greater good. They are also excellent communicators and empathizers ("Type Nine," n.d.).

Average Level

Level four mediators frequently exhibit more fear than healthy-level mediators. People pleasers are people who will often do what other people want, even if it is the opposite of what they want. This is because one of their greatest fears is conflict, so they are more at ease going with the flow (Cloete, n.d.).

At level five, type nine personalities begin to withdraw from the problems that surround them. They don't want to disengage, but they'd rather avoid the conflict. They also believe that ignoring the problem will make it go away on its own. They will begin to tune out people and their surroundings in order to avoid having to focus on what they believe is wrong. As a result, as they withdraw from society, they will begin to create a fantasy world for themselves ("Type Nine," n.d.).

Level six mediators will not completely ignore problems, but they will minimize them and try to bring some peace into their environment. They don't always care what the price is. They become obstinate and engage in magical thinking to help them solve problems that will make people happy.

Others, however, regard mediators at this level as uncaring, uninterested, and unresponsive (Cloete, n.d.).

Unhealthy Concentration

Level seven mediators believe they are incapable of dealing with the issues they face. As a result, they begin to drift away from their surroundings and society. As a result, they neglect themselves and can endanger themselves or others ("Type Nine," n.d.).

Level eight mediators will do anything to avoid seeing or hearing what they don't want to see or hear. They begin to become numb to the world around them at this point. In fact, they can become so disconnected that they struggle with day-to-day functioning (Cloete, n.d.).

At level nine, type nine personalities will develop various personalities to help them cope with the stress in their lives. Multiple personality disorder is the medical term for this. They become disoriented and unable to function in daily life ("Type Nine," n.d.).

Participation is a subtype of the Mediator Social Category.

The mediator is a well-known social butterfly. Because of their personality, they are usually very popular in their group setting. As participants, they do whatever they can to ensure the happiness of those around them, even if it means ignoring their own beliefs, stresses, and problems. They do this out of fear of becoming a burden. As a result, they frequently believe that it is best to deal with their problems on their own or to enlist the assistance of their closest friends and family. While they dislike burdening others, a healthy mediator recognizes that he or she cannot always deal with her problems alone and will seek assistance when necessary. Participation is regarded as the mediator's polar opposite (Cloete, n.d.).

Appetite is the Self-Preservation Category.

This type of mediator recognizes the importance of taking care of themselves in the same way that they take care of others. When type nine personalities have a lot of type eight personalities in them, they usually fall under this subtype. They want to ensure that everyone around them is happy and safe, including themselves. They believe they have found a healthy balance between caring for others, their surroundings, and themselves.

When people enter their reality and try to upset the balance they have created, they can quickly become upset, which is usually when they begin to form negative relationships with other personalities (Cloete, n.d.).

One-on-

Fusion is one of the categories.

This subtype of type nine personalities struggles to care for themselves as well as others. In fact, they believe that by assisting others, they are assisting themselves. In some ways, this works because the mediators gain pride and comfort from their actions when they

help others. This contributes to their desire to look after themselves. However, this is only applicable to a subset of their personal requirements. Unfortunately, because they want to focus more of their attention on others, type nine personalities in this subtype tend to ignore or push away their issues or feelings about certain things (Cloete, n.d.).

Relationships with People of Other Types

Any of the personality types can have a healthy relationship with the mediator. Because the mediator dislikes confrontation, he or she will often devise methods to avoid it. When confronted, however, they will try to do so in such a way that they do not cause emotional or physical harm to the other person. However, the manner in which they accomplish this is also determined by the mediator's level of integration ("Relationships (Type Combinations)," n.d.).

Center for Wings

The type one personality is one of the mediator's wings. The mediator's strengths include providing structure and focus over their perspectives, motivation to do what needs to be done, and offering support as the mediator works towards their goals. While mediators can take the time to ensure that their tasks are completed, the support and assistance of type one are critical in assisting them to complete these tasks (Cloete, n.d.).

Type eight is another wing type for the mediator. This type will empower the mediator by not only assisting them in becoming more active but also by providing them with a sense of power. Furthermore, the protector will provide the mediator with a sense of balance, allowing the mediator to develop into a unique individual rather than someone who follows the crowd. A type eight personality will also help the mediator become more confident and bold, allowing them to defend themselves when they feel threatened (Cloete, n.d.).

The Center of Attention

You are part of the body center if you have a type nine personality, and you will turn your anger into peace (Cloete, n.d.). This is why you are regarded as a peacemaker. You may find yourself simply ignoring things that irritate you in order to maintain harmony for yourself and those around you.

Strengths of type nine:
Non-judgmental
Caring
Approachable
Supportive
Excellent moderator
Adaptive \

Type nine's flaws include:

Indecisive
Forgetful
Stubborn \
Personal Development

Take Note of Your Emotions

Whether they are in a difficult situation or not, the mediator must be aware of their emotions. The more you understand that it is normal to feel these emotions, the less likely you are to try to disconnect from yourself, other people, and your surroundings. Furthermore, you will be able to achieve and maintain a healthy level of integration for your personality. This means you'll be able to face situations by imagining the best ways to overcome negativity in a peaceful manner, and you'll be able to carry on with your daily tasks to the best of your ability (Cloete, n.d.).

It is impossible to avoid conflict and negativity.

You must also maintain awareness of what is going on around you. While you don't want to dwell on the negative, it is a fact of life. It will be a part of your emotions, your surroundings, and the people who surround you. There is no way to avoid conflict and negativity entirely. These are factors that will assist you in maintaining a healthy level of integration if you learn to face them as you would any other. This will become easier once you realize you have the capability. Because of your peaceful nature, you have the ability to turn a negative situation into a positive one. If you want to withdraw from society because you are struggling, it is critical that you force yourself to stay on your path. To develop and improve your unique personality, you must confront your challenges, whether external or internal. This will help you become more mentally and emotionally engaged, which will only strengthen your abilities (Cloete, n.d.).

Learn to Recognize Your Body

You must not only become aware of your emotions, but you must also become aware of your body and how you control your emotions. For example, if you begin to exercise, you will become more aware of your body and how it responds to various exercises. You want to become more self-aware. This will not only help you maintain your cool during a crisis, but it will also allow you to think more clearly and focus more on yourself, others, and the environment. You'll be able to spot a problem before others do, which means you'll be able to diffuse the situation before it worsens (Cloete, n.d.).

Consider how you can help to solve problems.

No matter how hard you try to keep the peace, no one is perfect. It is critical for mediators to recognize that they are human and can make mistakes. For example, if you are having problems with your spouse, you should take a step back and examine why these problems are occurring. You must consider not only what you believe your spouse is doing incorrectly, but also how you contribute to the problem. Of course, this will be difficult, especially for a mediator. However, it is necessary if you want to truly solve the problem in a peaceful manner (Cloete, n.d.).

CHAPTER 11

Testing

The only way to truly determine your personality type is to take the Enneagram test. This test is easily accessible online or through a professional. The Enneagram test can be found at Eclectic Energies Enneagram Tests, which provides the test for free.

The Enneagram Institute also offers the test.

Concerning the Exam

The Enneagram test will ask you a series of questions and then tell you which personality type you are based on your responses.

These are simple questions that focus solely on your personality. For example, the test may ask you if you consider yourself to be an overall happy person and then rate your level of happiness or unhappiness.

While there are several versions of the test, each with a different number of questions, the results are usually fairly accurate. The results will show you a list of personalities and how much influence they have on you. You will also be given your primary personality type, secondary personality type, and so on. As a result, you will discover which personality type you are least likely to possess.

This test, however, will not only tell you what type of personality you have; it will also provide you with a detailed examination of other aspects of your personality that you have already learned about in several chapters of this book. You will, for example, discover whether you have a healthy, average, or unhealthy level of integration. You'll also discover your two wing centers, center point, and subtypes. At the same time, you'll get a sense of which personalities you relate to the most and which ones you'll struggle to get along with.

A summary of the nine types and subtypes

Because I've already gone over the nine personalities and their subtypes in-depth, I'm not going to go over them again in this section.

However, I recognize that this book contains a lot of information, which can be overwhelming. As a result, I wanted to take a moment to provide you with a brief summary of the last nine chapters you just read.

The perfectionist personality type is well-known. This is due to their desire to keep everything in order and to perform admirably at all times. Worry, zeal, and non-adaptability are the three subtypes of the perfectionist.

The helper is the second personality type. This will be their primary focus in life due to their desire to assist others. However, this can also be their fault because they tend to overlook their own needs.

Ambition, privilege, and seduction are their three subtypes.

The achiever is the third personality type. People with this personality are driven to achieve great success. Prestige, security, and charisma are their three subtypes.

The individualist is the fourth personality type. This personality type is known to be highly sensitive and strives to be their authentic self, even if it means hiding it from a crowd. Shame, tenacity, and competition are their subtypes.

The investigator is the fifth personality type. They are well-known for their attention to detail. They want to know as much as they can about a situation and their surroundings and will spend a significant amount of time attempting to figure things out. Totem, castle, and confidence are their three subtypes.

The loyalist is the sixth personality type. They are given this name because they are trustworthy. Duty, warmth, and intimidation are their primary subtypes.

The enthusiast is the seventh personality type. They are known to be outgoing individuals who see the best in everyone and everything. They are full of energy and optimism. Sacrifice, network, and fascination are their three subtypes.

The eighth personality type is known as the protector for a reason. They are known for their strength, resourcefulness, and fierce protection of their environment. Possession, solidarity, and satisfaction are their three subtypes.

The mediator/peacemaker personality type is the ninth and final personality type.

This personality type is non-confrontational and will do anything to keep the peace around them. Participation, appetite, and fusion are the mediator's three subtypes.

Difference between the Myers-Briggs Type Indicator and the Enneagram

There are numerous personality tests available to you.

The Enneagram and the Myers-Briggs are two of the most popular (Drenth, n.d.). The differences between the two tests will be discussed in this section.

Nature versus Culture

One of the most significant distinctions between the two tests is that the Myers-Briggs focuses on nature, whereas the Enneagram focuses on nurture (Drenth, n.d.). The Enneagram is more concerned with the events of your childhood. For example, your childhood experiences, both good and bad, will shape your personality as an adult. In fact, detailed reports on the personalities will frequently outline whether your adult problems are the result of your mother or father.

The Myers-Briggs test determines your personality type based on when you were born. While external factors can influence your personality, this test claims that some aspects of your personality have been with you since birth (Drenth, n.d.).

Unhealthy versus Healthy

One of the most striking aspects of the Enneagram is that each of the nine personalities has different levels of integration, ranging from healthy to unhealthy. According to the Enneagram, these levels will continue to develop in your personality throughout your life experiences. The Myers-Briggs test also considers psychological levels that are unhealthy or healthy. However, according to the Myers-Briggs test, you can have both a dominant and an inferior level. While you are aware of both of these levels in your personality, you are not aware of your inferior level as well as your dominant level (Drenth, n.d.).

CONCLUSION

You should be able to explain the Enneagram theory to anyone by now. You understand not only their basic personality traits, but also their healthy, average, and unhealthy levels. You can also identify their wing points, and how they form relationships with other personalities, subtypes, and center types. With all of these pieces, you can not only identify your personality type but also assist others in taking the test and explaining their personality types. There is a wealth of additional information available about the Enneagram theory. This book provided an in-depth examination of the theory; however, you can learn more about yourself and others by conducting additional research on the Internet or by reading other books. People enjoy learning as much as they can about a topic that interests them, as demonstrated by many of the personalities.

After reading this book, you should be able to not only take the test and determine which personality you have but also which level of integration you are on and what types of relationships you are capable of forming. It is critical to do everything possible to become the best person you can be, especially as you gain a better understanding of your personality.